Irresistible

HOW TO ENGAGE KIDS AND POINT THEM TO JESUS

Irresistible: How to Engage Kids and Point Them to Jesus
published by Kidmin Academy
edited by Tina Houser
copyright ©2018

cover design by Vanessa Mendozzi

CONTENTS

INTRODUCTION

I HAVE A FASCINATING little device (toy) called an energy stick that has served as after-dinner entertainment, an object lesson for kids, a focus in teacher training, and as a stocking stuffer. It's such a fun thing to play with! The energy stick is a clear tube with some wires running through it. When you touch one band at one end of the stick with your right hand, and grasp the other band at the other end of the stick with your left hand, the magic happens. The wires inside the tube light up in several colors and it makes an interesting, annoying little sound, because the circuit has been completed. But, it's not just a one-person toy. When others hold hands and grasp the ends of the energy stick, the same thing happens because the circuit has been completed. The unofficial record for number of people involved to complete an energy stick circuit is 1,113! It only takes one person, though, to let go of their neighbor's hand for the connection to break .. lights out ... silence.

The reason you've picked up this book is because you want the lights to come on in the kids you ministry to. You want the circuit to be complete. You want them to connect to God and His Word. You want to engage them at the highest level in a multitude of ways, so they will make the most important decision of their life—to begin a lifelong experience with The God of the Universe.

Within these pages, you'll gather information about how to get the attention of kids, how to relate to them, how to understand the way they think, how to encourage them to take personal steps toward God, how to effectively present the Bible ... all for the overarching goal of Engaging Kids. I encourage you to digest the content of each chapter to see how it fits into your plan of Engaging Kids with Jesus as their Savior and Lord.

If you're like me, you want more than an a-ha moment. You want an a-ha lifetime for your kids! That means that you need to learn how to use the tools that will engage them in worship, in healthy godly relationships, in the stories God has chosen to be in His Word, and in holy habits like scripture memorization, journaling, serving, daily devotions, and prayer. You want a connection to be made and the lights to come on! So, let's get started to see what your fellow kidmin leaders suggest in the chapters they have written.

Whether you're reading this book trying to figure out how to engage one challenging child, or you're wanting to step up your game as a large group leader, please know that these pages have been prayed over many times. That blanket of prayer is twofold: (1) that you will successfully lead kids in a spiritual engagement, and (2) that the kids will be receptive to making their own personal connection with God.

In His incredible joy,

Tina Houser

chapter 1

WILDLY PRECIOUS

Engaging Kids with Who They Are in God's Sight

BY KRISTY MOTTE

I'LL LET YOU IN on a little secret: although I love children's ministry, I spent almost a third of my life in the trenches with teens, neck deep in youth ministry. I wasn't avoiding a call; on the contrary, I was (joyfully!) responding to the call to be a helpmeet for my husband—then youth pastor, now family pastor. While children's ministry for me has been more confined to weekend and midweek gatherings, youth ministry often stretched far beyond the church's four walls. I spent countless hours (and still do) on couches, in coffee shops, or sitting on the floor of any available quiet corner listening to teen girls pour their hearts out ... hearts that were often empty, bruised, battered, or broken.

These teens confessed deep wounds inflicted by others or themselves. They confessed struggles with sin or addiction. Often they ran to the arms of the first available person who would have them, only to return feeling used and mistreated. Each time, I sat and listened while praying for the Holy Spirit to give me anything He could to comfort these girls. I asked for the right words to let them know that they are loved, not only by me, but by a Heavenly Father who is wild about them.

How did those teens get to that point? What is the difference between them and the bouncy, happy-go-lucky, sometimes crazy kids you work with each week?

Unfortunately, not much ... that is, unless you step in. The message each of those teens had failed to latch onto was who they were in God's sight. They knew who Jesus was and many had already surrendered their lives to Christ. But their hearts didn't really understand how valuable or worthwhile they were to God. They didn't know that their worth didn't come from making right choices, their talents, or because of their intelligence or good looks. They didn't understand that their Heavenly Father didn't view them the way their earthly father, mother, friends, teachers, or even church leaders did. They didn't know that God's view of them didn't change based on their grades that week or how well they did rejecting temptation.

What each one of those teens and what each of your children's ministry kids needs to understand is that their Heavenly Father is head over heels for them. He loves them with an everlasting love (Jeremiah 31:3) that is without conditions. Even beyond His love, they must understand that His love is the lens He sees them through. If they understood who they are in God's sight, they wouldn't be looking for acceptance in the world's sight.

This is where you, kidmin leader, paid or volunteer, come in. It's time you engage kids in who they are in God's sight. I propose that without that understanding of who they are in God's sight—beyond just head knowledge to a heart conviction they live out—kids are missing a foundation stone to their faith.

Without it, their acceptance of grace, unconditional forgiveness, and even their ability to seek the will of God is in jeopardy. Stick with me as we look at who kids are in God's sight, how you can adopt His view of them as your own, and then at how you can really engage kids in it, so they start seeing themselves as He does.

You could never exhaust who you are to God in one short chapter, so let's begin by taking a mile-high look. How does God see your kids?

MADE INTENTIONALLY BY THE FLAWLESS HANDS OF THE EXPERT CRAFTSMAN

I think as kidmin leaders, you do a great job making sure kids know that people were made by God. After all, you cover creation on a two-year cycle. Children understand that God made the world, including Adam and Eve, but sometimes you fail to convey the intentionality of the Creator and each child's individual importance to Him. To really understand who they are in God's sight, kids need to know that they personally were made by the flawless hands of The Expert Craftsman. His work is on purpose, without blemish, and for a purpose.

As you engage kids in who they are in God's sight, you want them to know that they were made in God's own image (Genesis 1:27). God saw fit to give them a spark of the divine, a reflection of who He is, as His creation. They should know that God knit them together by His own hand (Psalm 139:13-15), shaped each and every part of their physical form, and designed who they are, like a potter shapes clay (Isaiah 64:8). God sees them as His masterpiece (Ephesians 2:10), like His work of art. They should know that He made them because He has amazing plans for their lives (Psalm 139:16; Jeremiah 1:5; Ephesians 2:10). God placed each and every little boy and little girl here on purpose for a purpose.

THE HEAVENLY FATHER IS WILD ABOUT HIS CREATION

As you engage kids in who they are in God's sight, you want them to know He is wild about them. You want them to know that on their best days, their worst days, when they maybe don't even like themselves, their Father in Heaven is absolutely crazy about them! The Bible says He loves them deeply (1 John 4:9-10), they are on His mind, and His thoughts about them are precious (Psalm 139:17). What if a kid really grasped onto the idea that even when they are at their worst, God loves them more than anyone else ever could (Romans 5:8; John 15:13)? What if they really believe that nothing could change His view of them or separate them from His love (Romans 8:35-39)?

FULLY FORGIVEN, FULLY FREE

Perhaps one of the most difficult things for anyone to grasp is the idea that once you choose to follow Jesus, God doesn't see your sin anymore (Romans 5:1). Even children can find themselves defined by their struggles or the wrong they've done. But that's not who they are to God! When they've trusted in the redemptive work of the cross, God has cleansed even the deepest, darkest recesses of who they are (1 John 1:9). When I was in college, there was a certain set of boys' dorms that were known for being "the worst" on our Christian campus. There were several times a year that pranks went awry and the janitor was seen with a hose and a squeegee. He went into those dorms and sprayed them down from top to bottom. Then he squeegeed all the water back out; even the grossest dorms were fresh and clean again. God is far better equipped than any clean-up crew and promises that He cleans out even the grossest, grimiest, most hidden sin when you trust in Christ (Ephesians 1:7; Isaiah 1:18; Psalm 51:7).

Furthermore, God promises that when you belong to Him, He never sees your sin again (Psalm 103:12; Hebrews 10:17).

He sees you fully forgiven and fully made right with Him because of His Son. Kids need to know that there's no reason for guilt or condemnation with Christ. As long as they confess their sin to God, He never sees you in the lens of your sin; rather, He sees you as His precious masterpiece. There is so much freedom in that! I believe it's a freedom that God wants even the young to walk in. You're never too young to know that despite your wretched sin and inability to be perfect, God forgives, time and time again, even though it's undeserved.

When you realize that you're fully forgiven and fully free from the guilt and shame the enemy likes to use to chain you to your sin, you are then able to walk as the new creation God intended you to be (2 Corinthians 5:17). Kids can trust in the Craftsman's intentional work and walk in who He is calling them to be. It's there they begin to thrive and experience the Holy Spirit at work in and through them. I'm convinced that when that happens, they'll never look back!

So maybe you haven't learned anything new at this point. Of course, you know that God loves each and every child. You know He has a plan for their lives. But the next step in engaging kids in who they are in God's sight is adopting God's view of those kids as your view of them, too.

Hypothetically speaking, it's pretty easy to sit and think of an imaginary kid and agree with God's view. If you're like me, when my children were born, I couldn't help but humbly sit in awe of what God had entrusted me with, praying for His guidance as I feebly tried to provide opportunities that would shape them into who He made them to be. Babies are definitely lovable, special, forgivable, and let's face it, just down right cuddly. Now turn that baby into the first grader who comes in on Sunday like a tornado, after eating donuts for breakfast, and not sleeping much the night before. You know the one—can't keep their hands to themselves, wrecks your craft supplies so not even the other kids can enjoy them, derails the lesson at pivotal moments, or says just the right words to get under your skin. Do you see "that kid" like God sees them? This is where the rubber meets the road!

You see, the thing that makes God's view of you so amazing is that you just flat out don't deserve it. He sees you the same whether you spiral out of control like your (fully hypothetical, *a-hem*) mini-tornados or if you sit quietly with rosy cheeks that can't wait to be snuggled. Adopting God's view of the children you serve means you never base your view of your kids on their merit, actions, behavior, or attitudes. I'm not saying there won't be consequences when those things are out of line, but even your discipline then is shaped in a view that allows it to heal rather than hurt.

When you adopt God's view of the kids He has entrusted to you in ministry as your own, you are better equipped to lavish grace, readily forgive, joyfully clean, and even explain the same instructions for the fortieth time with a smile. I know ... easier said than done. In fact, on your own, I think it's probably impossible. It requires two things. First, it requires an understanding of how God sees you personally. When you really grasp that yourself, you are more prepared to bestow that same grace on others. And secondly, a whole lot of prayer! Ask the Lord to give you His eyes for your kids, especially the hard ones. And in the moment, when that tornado is wreaking its havoc, pray even more! Ask for His help to respond graciously and to love wholeheartedly. Ask Him to reveal the needs of the hearts of your children so that you never forget why your response is worth it.

So, how do you engage kids in who they are in God's sight? Now that you've adopted God's view of your ministry kids as your own, minister to them with that view in mind. In education, this is called your philosophy of teaching. It's the lens that drives your teaching and the outcomes you intend your classes to achieve. For kidmin leaders, it's your philosophy of ministry. You shape every lesson you teach, every craft you organize, every game you play, and every event that you run, around the hope that kids will fully understand how God sees them and the response He desires they have to the Gospel.

Practically speaking, what can you do?

Treat every child like they're today's guest of honor. Greet them enthusiastically. Let them know that you're glad they're there. Make sure they feel welcome and that they have everything they need. You can't do this alone so enlist the help of volunteers to do this with you as kids arrive each and every week.

Look for opportunities to praise. Praise effort, not just ability. Praise perseverance and progress. Praise good choices and good attitudes. Make it a goal that no child leave without at least hearing one time, "I'm so proud of the way you ..." or "I love the way God made you ..."

Accept unconditionally. Make sure every child knows they're welcome and loved, even on their worst days. It's okay to tell them, "You know, it seems like maybe you're having a rough day, but I am so glad you're here!"

Forgive and Forget. Don't ever make kids feel like you're keeping a record of their wrongs. Don't hold their mistakes against them or assume the worst because they've done it before. Never allow their bad behavior to define them. ("Oh, that's Miranda. Watch out, she's a runner.")

Never stop telling them about God's view of them. You can never tell someone too many times, "God loves you and so do I." Make sure they know God knows they struggle; God knows they experience hurt; God knows they have bad days. But He loves them just the same. And He wants to use even those hard things as part of His purpose for their life.

"Research shows that we tend to act in harmony with what we perceive ourselves to be. And often we allow our perception of ourselves to be based entirely on how others treat us" (S. Bell, "Mistaken Identity: See Yourself as God Sees You"). Let's aim to engage kids in who they are in God's sight, so that their perception is the same as their Heavenly Father's and their actions can follow.

Kristy Ann Mott is blessed to serve as the Elementary Children's Director of the Rock Church of Fenton alongside her incredible husband. She's the mom of 3 kiddos (ages four and under), a doctoral candidate (EdD at Liberty University), and online college instructor (and maybe just a little crazy).

chapter 2

A FIFTH GRADER'S POWERPOINT

Engaging the Voice of the Child

BY LACI CLIFFORD

T HERE I SAT, face-to-face with a near empty summer camp sign-up page. I was hunched behind my computer desperately hoping that God would cause some sort of electronic fish and loaves miracle to happen when I hit refresh. As I suspected, no such luck. There had always been some ebb and flow to summer camp registration, but the last three years seemed to have a lot more ebb and a lot less flow. Excuses felt like good medicine in the moment, so I quickly told myself that camp was so overrated and that I had done all that I could to build excitement. I had, after all, crafted some of my best social media posts, flooded parent inboxes with awesome photos and recap videos from previous years, and paraded every chaperone who was willing through our large group time to tell kids how great camp was. If we had to stop going to camp, then so be it. Eventually, the excuses stopped working and I had to admit that camp was still a huge catalyst for life transformation and, though I couldn't identify it yet, something was missing in our approach to telling children and families about it. Luckily, God is awesome, and He was preparing that miracle after all.

About a week later, I received an e-mail from a mother in our ministry with a PowerPoint presentation attached. When I opened it, I discovered a beautiful slideshow her fifth grade daughter had made about how awesome summer camp was. I immediately invited the daughter to come and share her presentation during our large group time. She was excited about the opportunity and, on the day of her presentation, she stood up in front of the group with confidence and walked them through each one of her slides. The children were riveted. They all sat on the edge of their seats leaning in over their knees towards the front so that they didn't miss any of the details. At the end of the presentation they were full of questions. The excitement was so high that you could feel it when you walked through the hallway. The children didn't stop talking about camp until the very last child had left the building that day.

I was so proud of her that I didn't even think about the camp sign-up page until the next morning. When I opened my e-mail, I couldn't believe what I saw. Six children who had never been to camp before signed up that night! Every day for the next week, more and more children signed up for camp until finally we had to create a wait list. By the time it was all said and done, we took 25% more children to camp than we had originally signed up for. That's 25% more children who got to hear the life transforming message of the Gospel. Now that really was a miracle!

It turns out that the piece I was missing didn't come through more e-mails, better social media posts, or even from the senior pastor saying something about my event from the pulpit, even though those are all good things. It came when I asked a child to participate in helping me get more children excited about going to camp. And, it wasn't just a happy accident. When

I applied what I learned about inviting children to participate to my planning and communication strategies in other areas, I was surprised to learn that children's engagement level went up significantly, although, it shouldn't have been a shock. After all, the value of children's input is a lesson you can see woven throughout scripture (Naaman's servant girl, anyone?) Engaging children by asking for their input is a way the church can speak powerfully to young people by showing them that they are cared for and important just the way God created them.

First, it connects them to adults who care. You can't know the interests, talents, or ideas of children without getting to know children and that builds relationships. It shows children that there are adults who truly want to know what they think and who value their opinion. Second, it allows them to explore possibilities. When children's ideas are heard, valued, and put into action it gives them confidence to discover things about themselves that they might not know. They might find that they can lead worship, serve others in creative ways, or start a neighborhood Bible study. Third, it gives them ownership. When children help plan and create something, they are more likely to fully participate in it and tell their friends about it.

Engaging children by asking for their input has other positive side effects too. Engaged children are usually excited children and excitement piques interest. Think about the last restaurant you ate in that was truly delicious. Or the last coupon you discovered that saved you a lot of money. Or the last gadget you found that now you can't live without. Chances are, you've told quite a few people about it and, because of you, they've checked out something they might not have known about otherwise.

What if this was true of your children's ministry? What if it were a place that sought after the input of children and worked with them to put those plans into action in a way that caused them to be more engaged and more receptive to the Gospel? Full disclosure: it will look different for every ministry. It will be challenging, and you'll go through seasons of getting it more and less right. If you're ready to get messy, have fun, and discover new things, here are a few ways to start.

START SMALL

Let's face it. You all serve in children's ministry in some capacity and therefore have a tendency to get really excited about things. Like, the kind of excited that makes you dye your hair for contests or believe you can stuff thousands of eggs with candy and toys in a few short hours. However, don't skip into your large group room on Sunday morning and ask all of your elementary kids what they want to do next in the ministry. I can imagine that you would get some awesome ideas about turning the whole church into a swimming pool or replacing all the goldfish with cotton candy. With a group that size working on it, you'd never be able to turn it into a reality. Choose a few interested children or a specific small group to talk with first, get ideas from, and make a plan for what the next step might be.

ASK GOOD QUESTIONS

Don't get yourself stuck in a situation where "I don't know. What do you want to do?" loops more times than your favorite roller coaster. Think about exactly what you want to know and ask questions that might help you get there with the age group you're working with. If your team wants to know how to get children excited about coming to church on Sunday morning and inviting their friends, you might ask questions like, "What's your favorite thing we've ever done at church?" and, "What kinds of things do you and your friends like to do together?"

RELEASE SOME CONTROL

To be honest, if I had created the PowerPoint presentation from my summer camp story it might have looked a lot different. I probably would have taken some of the details she focused on out or talked about elements of the camp in a different way. But that's the beauty of asking children for their input. You get to see the unique way that God created them and oftentimes they see things in a way that you don't. That sweet fifth grader paid careful attention to highlight the details she knew would matter to her peers like: what tracks were outside vs. inside, what meals were worth being the first in line for, and what the most important thing to bring to camp is (a flashlight, by the way). It might not be how you would do it, but if you're intentional about listening and working together you'll find that God can use your group, no matter the ages represented, to do some amazing kingdom work.

THINK OUTSIDE THE BOX

A few years ago we had a young man in our mid-week program who did not want to be there and was therefore disengaged during activities. When the team's focus was on his lack of participation in the group, it made matters worse. Then, one of the leaders started asking him questions and learning about his interests. Eventually, it led to a conversation about photography and how he would like to take pictures of some of the projects the group was doing. He had great ideas about what pictures to take and how to show them to the parents of the children in his group. The leader worked with him to help him make his idea happen. Consequently, our mid-week program became a place where he thrived and he learned about the unique perspective and talent God had given him as he looked through the lens of a camera. If that leader hadn't thought outside the box and been willing to ask questions and get his input about how he might get excited about participating, he would have never been engaged.

EMBRACE THE ORGANIC

Remember to bring your listening ears to every conversation that you have with a child. Admittedly, five sections with bold titles can seem like all of this input you are receiving from children has to be done in a formal way. It can be. You can have a plan, make a list of questions, and have an end in mind. But if that's all you do, you might just miss the big ideas in the little moments. Listen in the down times—while you're driving the van to a retreat, while you're waiting in line for food, when you're doing an activity with a few early arrivers. Think about what your children are doing, saying, and engaging with outside of the walls of your church. Give children space to talk and space to dream. Help them discover who God created them to be so that they can be fully engaged in His story.

Asking children for their input and ideas is one of those things that you know is true as adults. After all, doesn't everyone like to be asked for their thoughts on things? It is a way that you make others feel special, valued, and respected. It's no different with the children in your ministry.

Somewhere deep inside you know that, but it gets lost. It gets buried under our massive to-do lists that somehow never get smaller. It gets hidden behind the false message you sometimes let yourself believe that as a leader you should know all the answers or generate the ideas. It gets missed in the routine of how it's always been done or the flashy allure of the next big thing. But what would happen if you dug deeply and truly prioritized the creativity that God has given to each person, including children? What if you pulled back the curtain of false messages you let yourself believe about leadership? What if you focused on the precious people that God put in front of you today and listened to really hear what might engage the next generation?

I am so thankful for that PowerPoint. God used it to remind me of the importance of helping children use their voice. He took the gifts He had given that fifth grade girl and used them to engage her peers in a way that drew them to camp and ultimately closer to Him. Children are important and they matter to God. When you engage them by asking for their input and invite them to participate you are giving them a glimpse into just how much they are loved and cared for by their Heavenly Father. And I'm excited to engage in that!

Layci Clifford is the Minister to Children at a church in Northern Virginia. She believes that kids don't have to wait to be used by God and enjoys creating experiences that help kids discover that.

chapter 3

A GAME OF DARTS

Engaging Kids According to How They are Wired

BY BRITTANY NELSON

THINK OF CHILDREN'S MINISTRY like a game of darts. You want what you're teaching (the darts) to stick with the children you are teaching (the dartboard). Engaging children according to how they are wired developmentally and relationally allows you to take better aim and hit the bullseye. Trying to teach a preschooler an abstract concept of faith would be like trying to throw the dart backward and hoping it sticks. It may leave an imprint, but will, for the most part, miss the mark completely. Knowing and understanding how children are uniquely wired for learning, technology, and relationships helps you be more effective in your presentation of biblical truths and allows you to combine theology and scientific theory to create the most well-rounded approach to ministry and sharing the Gospel.

WIRED FOR LEARNING

Developmentally, kids are wired for learning. The speed at which their little brains absorb and process new information is unlike any other stage of life. This is great news for you! Their minds are already ready for the truths you want to teach them. But that doesn't mean every child is developmentally ready for every truth. While children may progress through stages of learning at different rates, they tend to follow the same patterns of development from birth to the preteen years, and when you engage kids based on their developmental stage, you can take better aim at the dartboard. Use the chart below to gain a general overview of a child's characteristics in each stage and what that means for a practical application to ministry.

Age/Stage of Life	Characteristics of Developmental Stage	Practical Application
Nursery (Infant-Toddler)	Physical observations important for learning Learning to trust through relationships with parents and caretakers Sense of self-autonomy and independence begins to develop in toddlerhood	Model habits and spiritual disciplines Respond to needs quickly Create safe environments Offer opportunities to make decisions, no matter how small Offer events and activities that build relationships

Preschool & Young Elementary	Creative and emotional learning; imaginative play is the most common form of learning Influenced by images, stories, and symbols Logical thinking is not yet present (which is why you can never win an argument against a pre-schooler) Beginning to develop self-worth based on how useful, purposeful, and competent they feel	Incorporate imaginative play often Use images and stories in Bible teaching Provide ways for children to serve and be active participants in each activity Offer events and activities that build relationships
Older Elementary	Thinking concretely; literal interpretations of Bible stories Beginning to think logically and look for order in the world, but still find meaning in stories Becoming aware of their individuality and uniqueness	Connect the lesson to something children interact with on a weekly basis (use object lessons) Be prepared to answer logical, black-and-white questions Recognize and celebrate what makes each child unique Offer events and activities that build relationships

Preteen	Abstract thinking emerges	Go deeper with theological ideas
	Starting to question their faith as it becomes their own	Create a trusting environment where preteens feel comfortable asking questions
	Can begin to see the perspective of others	
	Fitting into a community and with their peers increases in importance	Provide more missions opportunities
	Beginning to form their own philosophy of life and faith and how they themselves fit into their budding worldview	Offer events and activities that build relationships

If you want to read more about developmental stages and how they influence spiritual formation in children, I recommend the book *Christian Formation: Integrating Theology and Human Development* by James Estep and Jonathan Kim.

WIRED UNIQUELY

While kids develop through these stages in roughly the same process, *how* they develop depends on each one's unique personality and learning style. A social learner will need to talk about what she is learning to best understand it, but a solitary learner will prefer to work and think alone. A physical learner will need hands-on experience with the idea, while a verbal learner might need to write out the idea in his own words. You tend to teach the way you prefer to learn, so be aware of your own learning style so you can ensure a balance of teaching methods in your ministry. If you treat all learners the same, you invite boredom-induced chaos.

Being aware of the different learning styles and personalities of the children you serve will help you better engage them each week. Allowing children to interact with the day's lesson in a variety of ways will help ensure you give each type of learner the opportunity to shine. One of my favorite ways to do this is through stations. Most curriculums offer a large-group, small-group format for Sunday mornings, but as a mobile church with limited time, space, and resources for creating an exciting environment, I had to come up with a way to make our mornings more engaging for kids.

So I adapted the big-name curriculum we were using to fit a new format: large-group time, then stations. Kids loved it! Rather than small groups completing all of the activities in one place, small groups rotate between the activities set up as four stations: Snack, Experience, Play, and Create. When converting the big-name curriculum I used, I went through and picked out an activity I thought would fit each station and adjusted the instructions a little. Each station is designed to cater to a different learning style and to allow children to use a different part of their brain to interact with the Bible story/main lesson. Stations allow more movement throughout the morning and mean that you need fewer supplies since only one small group will be doing the activity at a time. Since each station lasts 10 minutes, that one kid who hates crafts knows that a new activity is coming soon, so it helps eliminate disengagement.

At Snack, children enjoy a snack while discussing response and review questions about the day's Bible story or main lesson. A small group activity or Bible memory verse activity accompanies this station, and if your curriculum provides Bible story videos, this is the perfect place to use those.

At Experience, children participate in a science experiment, object lesson, or prayer activity that makes our Bible lesson tangible while also inciting wonder and amazement. Experience is designed to give the "deep thinkers" the chance to connect the way things work in our world to the lessons God has for us in the Bible.

At Play, children have the chance to run around in a high-energy game or compete against each other in some type of relay race. Play is designed to give children the opportunity to expel some of their energy in an exciting way while also building friendships, promoting teamwork, and connecting real-life games to the Bible lesson.

At Create, children use their artistic, creative, or theatrical skills to make a craft, group project, or re-enactment of the Bible story, and it's a great place for all of the creative thinkers and artists to use some of the talents God has given them.

Using stations, or at least evaluating the types of activities your children complete on a Sunday morning, can help increase your aim when throwing the darts. Because you engage them in the unique way that God designed them, kids are more excited about learning and therefore more receptive to the teaching.

WIRED FOR TECHNOLOGY

Technology often gets a bad rap, but it's not going anywhere, and if you don't work to leverage technology for the advancement of the Gospel, you will grossly miss your targets. Today's kids don't know a world without the existence of technology and the internet. The Barna Group found that children spend an average of five hours on an electronic device (tablet, phone, computer, etc.) every day (barna.com/research/6-tech-habits-changing-american-home/). As a ministry leader, you have to use technology in your ministry to engage kids in what you are teaching and how it can apply to their lives. If you aren't using technology in your ministry in some way, you'll lose kids (and their parents), because they'll subconsciously view the church as outdated and irrelevant. Kids interact with technology on a daily basis anyway, so why not redirect some of that screen time to be part of the discipleship process? Here are some simple ways to incorporate technology into your ministry.

Screen or Video-Led Games. There are thousands of video or PowerPoint-led games you can use during large-group time or parent pick-up. Check out YouTube or Worshiphousekids. com for some great ideas. During one of our space-themed units, I used a "space race" video that encouraged kids to choose a colored rocket ship and cheer for that one during a 30-second on-screen race. Each time, a different color won. This game quickly became a favorite pick-up time activity, and it matched our unit theme, helping kids remember the overall idea.

Bible Story Videos. Most of the popular curriculums provide videos with their lessons, so use these videos as a supplement to your in-person teaching. I'm a firm believer that the Bible story should be taught by a person first, then reinforced with technology. That way, kids hear the story at least twice and in two different formats. If your curriculum does not provide videos, look around online or make your own. The possibilities are endless.

Worship. If you're one of the lucky children's pastors who has a full band to lead worship, just skip ahead to the next idea. If you're like the rest of us, you can use exciting lyric videos during worship to engage kids with technology. Again, Worshiphousekids.com is a great place to start your search. Using lyric videos also allows you to share the videos with your families so they can listen and worship at home, too. And if you enable your preteens to run slides/videos for you, that's a great way to engage them and give them opportunities to serve at the same time.

At-Home Activities. Equip the parents in your ministry with awareness of or access to biblical apps, games, and websites. Some of my families' favorites include AdventureBible. com, The Aetherlight (a biblical allegory computer game), and JellyTelly. You can also create videos or podcasts for families to listen to at home or in the car that remind them of the lesson, prepare them for what's next, and encourage discussion. Because the car is quickly replacing the dinner table as the family gathering place, providing resources kids and families can use on-the-go will remind them of the lessons each week and keep them engaged in the overarching story of the unit.

WIRED FOR RELATIONSHIPS

God wired us with a need for community as a reflection of His triune character, and the same holds true for children. Kids need relationships with their peers and with their leaders. Friendships are especially important in the preteen years. I've found that groups of sixth graders who enter the middle school youth group as friends tend to have an easier time transitioning than a group of students who don't feel close. Especially as preteens experience "11-year-old atheism" (when children have a difficult time reconciling an unknowable God with their concrete way of thinking), they need leaders they trust and peers they can learn with. Creating a community in which to doubt, play, and grow provides the healthiest environment for engaging children.

Learning is a social process in itself, so intentionally invite interaction and relationships in your ministry. It will help stimulate growth and engage kids in what you are teaching. Children's faith develops based on who they love and mimic, not what they do or know. So often, children's ministry can become about helping kids memorize Scripture and know the right answers. And while those things are important to a biblical faith foundation, the most vital thing is relationships with mentors and leaders in the Christian faith. Kids are more receptive to your teachings when they feel known and loved by you, so you have to take the time to build relationships with them outside of Sunday mornings if you want them to listen to you on Sunday mornings.

Kids cannot progress through life without the influence of positive relationships with both their parents and other adults. In nearly every aspect of how kids are wired at each stage of life, being exposed to challenges and different perspectives from others helps them move to the next stage of development. The presence of community is vital for overall spiritual growth, and when you use community to engage kids, your effectiveness increases.

HIT THE TARGET

As you build relationships with kids and learn who they are, you will be better able to identify their unique needs, preferences, and stages of life. When you engage kids based on their developmental level and according to their unique needs, your ministry becomes more effective. You're better able to aim the darts and hit your targets, ultimately fulfilling your purpose of engaging kids with God and the Bible.

Brittany Nelson is the creator of DeeperKidmin.com, an online resource that equips ministry leaders to grow kids deeper in their relationships with Christ through engaging and affordable ideas. In her spare time, she enjoys reading, chocolate, tea, and yoga, and she wants to someday run the Disney Princess Half Marathon dressed as her favorite princess, Belle.

chapter 4

APOLOGETICS FOR KIDS: THE WHAT, WHY, AND HOW
Engaging Children to Defend Their Faith

BY AMBER PIKE

CAN THE CHILDREN in your ministry answer basic faith questions about sin, Jesus, and salvation? They can probably tell you that Jesus is God's Son ... that He died on the cross, but after three days He rose from the dead ... that's awesome! Knowing and understanding basic foundational faith questions is huge. But what if you asked the children in your ministry *how* they know that Jesus didn't stay dead? Could they explain to someone *how* they know the Bible is true? Are they prepared to defend their beliefs?

The What - Apologia: (Greek) to give defense

Apologetics is the branch of theology devoted to the defense of Christianity. To put it simply, it is knowing what you as a Christian believe and how to defend it. The Bible tells you that you are to be prepared to give a defense (1 Peter 3:15). Give a defense of what, though?

The Word of God is on constant attack from the world around you. From the questioning of the existence of God to compromise on His Word. Both in the secular world and even within the church, Christianity and the Word of God are under attack. Our children are exposed to this attack on a regular basis. School textbooks contradict God's Word. Television shows and movies question and ridicule Christian values and even God Himself. The attack on God and His Word is everywhere you look, including in the lives of our children.

The Why – Why should children be taught apologetics?

Research has shown that two-thirds of young people are leaving the church. These studies have revealed that children are leaving the church, in part, because of the lack of answers. Oftentimes, children are not given the answers they seek. They are told they need to just trust in Jesus, or that their question doesn't matter, or the teacher simply doesn't know the answer and doesn't follow up with finding it. When no answers to their questions are provided, for whatever the reason, children begin to doubt God's Word. Doubt of God's Word leads to rejection of God and possibly to the eventual walking away from the faith.

If your goal is to see the children in your ministry have an authentic, lifelong relationship with Christ, then you need to engage your children in defending their faith. Thinking that children do not need to be taught how or are not capable of defending their faith, is a crucial mistake. Children are capable of understanding deep theological issues. They are capable of great understanding, even at a young age. They do not need a watered-down faith and are never too young to be taught large theological concepts. Start early on teaching children to defend their faith. When you teach children what they believe and how to defend it, and you give them the answers they need to the questions they ask, the likelihood they will have a lasting faith relationship with Christ increases.

Not only can apologetics help a child stay in a lifelong, authentic relationship with Christ, but it can benefit and strengthen other areas of their lives as well. Teaching apologetics to children can:

- Deepen their faith.
- Equip them to share their faith.
- Help them combat lies and attacks on God's Word.

When you spend time preparing to defend your faith to others, you are spending time with God learning what YOU believe.

The How – How do you equip children to defend their faith?

Teaching apologetics to children gives children the answers they need. Dismissed and disregarded questions can lead to doubt. Give kids the answers they need to strengthen their faith. But how do you do that?

- You need to start with the Bible.
- Show kids God's story of redemption running through the Bible.
- Answer the questions kids ask, and the ones they don't.
- Lastly, you need to educate, encourage, and equip parents at home.

START WITH THE BIBLE.

The Bible is the inspired, inerrant Word of God. God does not lie, so the Bible must be true. It is useful for teaching, correction, reproof, and training in righteousness (2 Timothy 3:16-17). Before you begin teaching apologetics and answering children's questions you must start on the foundation of the Bible. The Bible is the ultimate source of authority in your life and should be taught as such. The Bible is God-breathed. It is complete and free of errors. Teach it as such.

There is no room for compromise on God's Word. If you believe the Bible is wrong about one thing (like there being a literal worldwide flood), then the Bible cannot be trusted to be true about salvation. If the Bible is true in one area, it must be true in all areas. You cannot pick and choose which areas of the Bible to trust and follow. When you do that, when you allow compromise on the truth of God's Word, you allow doubt to open up the door to rejection of God's Word and to Christ as Lord and Savior. When teaching apologetics to children, you must start on the foundation of God's Word, on its inerrancy and sufficiency.

TEACH GOD'S STORY OF REDEMPTION.

The basic, foundational truths about God's Word are probably standards in your children's ministry. Your children are being taught that God wrote the Bible and that the Bible is true, but are they being taught the Bible as God's Story of Redemption for mankind? As one big God-Story? Look at the curriculum you are using in your children's ministry. Do the lessons hop around or does each lesson build on the previous one? With many curriculums, one week the kids learn about Moses and the next they are on Paul. When lessons hop around, kids are not able to grasp a big picture understanding of the Bible. They can't see the central theme running throughout the Bible or how the events and characters relate to Jesus. The Bible then becomes a collection of stories instead of God's one story of redemption for mankind.

Chronological Bible studies teach children how the whole Bible, how each story, fits into God's story of redemption. Show the children how the events in the Old Testament point to the need for and promise of the Savior, while the New Testament is the fulfilment of that promise. Help them understand that David wasn't just a good king, but how his kingdom relates to Christ. Show them the relationship between Joseph and Moses. Show children how the Bible accounts and characters connect not only to each other, but also how they fit into the context of the big God story in the Bible. Teach God's story of redemption.

ANSWER THE "BIG" QUESTIONS

"How did all the animals fit on the ark?" "Was Adam a real person?" "Are we really created in the image of God?" "Where did God come from?" "Isn't science true?" Kids have questions. The Holy Spirit might be moving in them as they grow spiritually causing their desire to learn and question. They could be questioning parts of the Bible that they aren't sure of. Maybe what they are being taught at school doesn't line up with what the Bible says and they need to figure out which one is true. Teaching the answers to these questions, and not compromising the Word of God, is so important. When children are told to not question things and just trust in Jesus, doubt and compromise are given an opening. Their questions need to be answered!

At first glance, questions about the age of the earth or the flood are not necessarily salvation issues. Not providing answers to these questions might not seem like a big deal. Will a person get to heaven if they do or do not believe in six literal days of creation? As long as Jesus is their Lord and Savior, yes. Belief in Christ Jesus is what saves a person, not their beliefs on apologetic related questions. Though it might not seem like a person's view on the flood or a literal Adam is a salvation related issue, apologetics for the sake of the Gospel is so important.

Not only can answering a child's questions satisfy their curiosity and strengthen their faith, but it can stop compromise on the Word of God for the sake of the Gospel. Look at the issue of a literal Adam. Scripture tells us the first man God created was a man named Adam. Yet some people believe there was not a literal first man named Adam. How is this a salvation issue? If there was not a literal first Adam, then there cannot be a literal last Adam, Jesus (1 Corinthians 15:45-49). If Adam did not exist, then Jesus who died on the cross to take on the sins of the world and offers us forgiveness and everlasting life, cannot exist. God would have lied and the Bible would contain errors. If God lied or the Bible contained errors, you could not trust that Jesus is the only way to heaven. A literal Adam then becomes a salvation issue, important for the sake of the Gospel.

These big, apologetic questions are, at their core, Gospel issues. When children bring questions to you, take the time to answer their questions, starting with what the Bible says about the issues. (Always start from the Bible!) What might seem like a trivial or unimportant question needs to be answered for the sake of the Gospel. Not only will it strengthen their faith and belief in the Bible, but it will give them the answers they need to defend and share their faith with others.

EDUCATE, ENCOURAGE, AND EQUIP PARENTS AT HOME.

You can regularly teach apologetics to the children in your ministry, but if you do not have the parents on board, you're fighting an uphill battle. Take the time to educate, encourage, and equip the parents in your ministry. Children are not only taking their questions about the Bible to you, but to their parents as well. Are the parents in your ministry equipped to answer these questions? Do they know the answers to their kid's questions or where to find them? Apologetic training should be a priority not just for the children in your ministry but for their parents as well.

Educate parents on what is being taught to their children. Take-home papers, emails, and newsletters are great for giving a brief overview and outline on what is being taught. For apologetic training though, consider taking it a step further. Inform and provide parents with the same apologetic teachings. Send out papers, emails, or videos explaining the "Big Questions" that were answered. Many Sunday school curriculums even offer the same curriculum for kids, youth, and adults. Parents know exactly what their children learned that day, because they had the same lesson in their adult class.

Offer parenting classes or workshops on the Bible. Some parents are afraid to admit that they do not have a strong foundation of biblical knowledge. If they don't understand or know God's Word, they are unable to teach their children how to defend their faith.

Send resources home. What tangible items can you put into parents' hands for them to use? Can you recommend or provide them with great chronological Bibles? Did you come across a great video you can share that will equip them? Are there any holiday resources or family devotions that can help families defend their faith?

Don't just assume that the parents in your ministry know how to defend their faith or are equipped to answer their children's questions. Make it a priority to educate, encourage, and equip parents on how to defend their faith as they lead their family.

RESOURCES YOU CAN USE

Below are some great resources and ideas to use as you engage children to defend their faith.

Resources for teaching God's Story of Redemption

- Answers Bible Curriculum – an apologetic based, chronological Sunday school style, 4-year curriculum (available for preschool through adult)
- What's in the Bible – 13 videos and curriculum providing foundational knowledge of the Bible and answers to tough questions as kids journey through the Bible
- The Big Picture Interactive Storybook Bible – a storybook Bible that connects each story to Christ

- Giant 10-ft. Bible Timeline – Hendrickson Rose Publishing

Practical Classroom Apologetics

- Question and Answer Time. Regularly schedule apologetics training.

- "I Don't Know." You are not expected to have an answer for every question. It's okay to say "I don't know." Follow that up, however, with "but I will find out." Make sure you follow through.

- Go Off Script. Some of the best lessons are the ones that are not written down. When the Holy Spirit is moving in a child's life and those wheels are turning in their head, they are going to have questions. Take the time to answer those questions and allow the Spirit to lead you.

- Question Them. Get the children thinking by presenting them with apologetic questions before they ask them. Provide them with the answers and resources they need to answer these questions.

Big Apologetic Issues

- Creation: length of days, how God created
- The Flood: local or global, animals on the ark, dinosaurs
- Science vs. the Bible
- Sin and suffering from a loving God
- Jesus: fully God and fully man, Last Adam, one way to heaven, resurrection
- One Race (Tower of Babel)
- The Bible: God-inspired, inerrant, complete, "contradictions"

Engage the children in your ministry to defend their faith. There is a war raging for the souls of your children. You want to see them walk in an authentic, lifelong relationship with the Savior. Teach them how to defend their faith. By taking the time to teach children what the Bible says, what Christians believe and why, will strengthen and solidify their faith. It gives them the answers they need, with the Bible as the foundation on which they build their lives. It increases the likelihood that they will not walk away from the faith, and it gives them the tools they need to defend their faith and share it with others. Do not allow doubt and compromise on the Word of God to enter your ministry. Start today, engaging your children to defend their faith.

Amber Pike is a children's minister, writer, wife, and mom of two in LaGrange, KY. She spends her days homeschooling, taking care of her family, and getting as much accomplished during the baby's nap time as possible!

chapter 5

SURFING WAVES AND TRAINING HORSES
Engaging Kids as Lifelong Worshipers

BY EMILY HILL

IF YOU'VE EVER TRIED incorporating praise and worship into the children's ministry at your church I would guess that there have been some challenges along the way. Some of the questions that my team has wrestled with are:

- How do you balance movement and excitement with adoration and prayer?

- How do you tell kids to be free in worship but still keep things under control?

- How do you engage an entire room of kids filled with different ages and personalities?

Let's dance our way through the answers to these questions.

GOING FROM CRAZY TO CALM

When planning your worship set list, it should have a natural flow to it that goes from energizing to transitional to calming. The idea is to have celebratory praise music that transitions into prayerful worship. Many kids naturally struggle with transition and if it's not handled correctly can lead to some unsavory behaviors that will distract from worship. Try to think of your worship set list visually as ocean waves.

Deep out in the ocean there are dominant surface waves that are big, loud, and cause a thrill to those on boats and surf boards. This should be the energy level of your opening worship songs. You want the worship at the beginning to get kids excited. They start tapping their feet, clapping their hands, and feeling the music coursing through their hearts. This is when you want to crank up the music and lead the kids through full body movement. Make sure you also have adults on your worship team who are able to let loose and show kids how it's okay to have fun while praising God.

As the waves head toward the beach they begin to slow down. These waves are still fun to ride with a jet ski, but you can also start to see what's beneath the waves. Mid-worship songs are an opportunity to keep some up-tempo songs while beginning to slow down movement. Focus on full arm gestures and guide their attention toward the meaning of the specific songs.

When waves reach the shore, they have calmed to the point of barely lapping against your ankles and have become so clear that you can see your toes. The final worship songs are an opportunity to slow down and reflect. These are not words typically used to describe a group of children, so don't be discouraged if this proves to be the most challenging transition. Take time to gather all of the kids together for a moment of prayer and then guide them into a song which has simple hand motions (hands raised, arms held open), which can help to frame the expectations for this portion of worship.

I AM FREE!

As my team began to incorporate worship into children's church the kids requested "I Am Free" every Sunday. Why? Because it was the first time many of them had been told to run and dance in church! You could see the pure joy on their faces as they ran around the room shouting "I Am Free." It was a beautiful thing ... until the song was over. The running and dancing continued, but what once seemed like joyful cheering now changed into something similar to a war cry. We spent the remaining worship time telling kids to "stop running" and "calm down." This didn't create a quality worship experience for anyone involved.

We all know that when kids get a taste of freedom, it's hard to bring them back from that and return to the actual environment. So I have the perfect solution: join them in their freedom. What? Okay, I'll say it again. Join them in their freedom.

Week after week, we persisted with "I Am Free." The kids loved it, right? What changed was the involvement of the adults in the room. Instead of watching the kids run and dance around the room, we joined them! We shared our faith by outwardly expressing praise to God and having fun while doing it. As the song came to a close, we found ourselves mixed in with the kids throughout the room. This was a huge advantage as the next song started because we could show, through our own actions, how to interact. The kids looked all around them to see how the adults were acting (how they should act). You'll still have those kids who take a little longer to slow down and ride those waves to the shore, but if you have a team of leaders who are willing and able to worship side by side with the kids it will make a huge difference.

JESUS LOVED THE LITTLE CHILDREN

"Then people brought little children to Jesus for him to place his hands on them and pray for them" Mark 19:13a (NIV).

As someone working with children on a regular basis, I find myself reading this scripture often with different perspectives. The picture paired with this verse is typically of Jesus surrounded by sweet-faced children, gazing at Him with adoration. I can only imagine what it would be like to glimpse the face of Jesus Christ as a child and I'm sure both them and their families were in awe of this man. However, while reading this verse, I often picture a couple children off to the side doing cartwheels, picking flowers, twirling around, and poking their neighbor. Let's be honest, our children today can't be that much different than those from biblical times!

No matter how hard you try to do the biggest, flashiest, and next best thing in worship with your children, there will still be those who are not going to stand with the group and do the motions along with the worship team, at least not right away. Your group of children may look different than mine, but my guess is that most of us have some kids who fall into similar types.

The Twirler. Twirlers love to do cartwheels and twirl in circles with arms spread wide and eyes closed. They seem to enjoy the beat of the music and often have the hardest time winding down for prayerful worship. Twirlers look like they're having lots of fun, so they usually attract an audience which leads to more twirlers. We have ended up going through periods of having a large group of twirlers in the back during worship. We decided to divide and conquer by creating large squares out of tape on the floor (think stretched out 4-square court) and giving each Twirler their own square. They can do whatever they like, but it can't leave the box and has to be quiet. This has allowed them to twirl, dance, twist, and turn in whatever ways they like that doesn't create an unsafe space for other worshipers.

The Talker. As soon as the worship music comes on, the talker suddenly has a very important conversation topic to discuss with everyone around them. Sometimes, they will talk so loud that you can hear them over the music. When our worship leader sees an extra chatty talker, she calls them up with her to pray and read scripture. Maybe singing isn't their thing; it doesn't work for everyone. Obviously, they enjoy talking, so we just give them a way to use it and add to the worship experience for everyone. We also engage them on the songs that have parts to yell or chant. This doesn't "count" as singing, so they're usually excited to jump in on these parts.

The Grump. You'll see the grump with arms crossed, leaning against a wall, and straight faced. I'm almost positive that we all have known a grump. They seem to have different reasons for being a grump (shy, new to class, too cool), but it all usually comes across the same way. No matter how silly you get, they will not crack a smile and definitely will not join in with you. To engage a grump takes time and trust; it will not happen overnight. Relationships must be built and you must move at their pace. When handling grumps in our ministry, try to pair them up with someone you think they could connect with and who loves worship. This could be an adult or another child. The classroom leaders are intentional about pairing them up during lesson activities and the idea is that they continue that connection during worship. It doesn't happen in a single Sunday, but is worth the effort to see this child connect with worship over time.

In regards to those children who may need accommodations due to physical or cognitive disabilities, finding what works for each individual child is always the best option. We had a child who was uncomfortable with the loud music and would just stand in the worship space with his hands covering his ears for weeks. After a lot of trial and error, discussions with parents, and caring leaders, he now worships with a couple adults in a separate room where he can still hear the music but it's at a comfortable volume for him. His parents couldn't believe it when he came home singing worship songs because he had never been able to tolerate concert-level music. We found something that worked for him and allowed him to enter into worship with others. These children have a high sensitivity to sound and headphones are another good option for them to utilize during periods of loud sound.

THIS AIN'T MY FIRST RODEO

Growing up, I attended some camps where we learned basic skills on how to work with horses. The main thing that stood out to me was that above and beyond everything else, training a horse was about building trust between the horse and the rider. That's not much different than working with children and helping them engage in worship. As a leader in their spiritual journey, children need to know they can trust you. By building trust in worship, they know that there are people in their lives whom they can come to when in need of guidance, someone to listen, or maybe just an extra hug.

To build trust with the horses, we were encouraged to spend time doing things that they enjoyed and bonding. Transitioning this into the idea of worshiping with children, you can also bond with them and build trust by doing things they enjoy. Whether you are the check-in greeter, preschool teacher, worship leader, or anything in between, take time to bond with the kids. Find out what they enjoy doing and then do it! Bring a fidget spinner to church, learn how to play Minecraft, start collecting Shopkins ... whatever it takes to connect with the interests of the children. When you bond with kids outside of worship, it allows you to connect with them on a deeper level during worship. They know you and they trust you.

Another valuable lesson learned from training a horse was to never get angry. Sure, they might do something that makes you upset, but you would instantly dissolve any trust you may have built by getting angry. It's appropriate to correct disrespect, but it should be done in a calm manner. As an adult, you know how important worship is in your relationship with God.

Scripture tells us, *"Praise him with the tambourine and dancing; praise him with strings and flutes! Praise him with a clash of cymbals; praise him with loud clanging cymbals. Let everything that breathes sing praises to the Lord! Praise the Lord!"* Psalm 150:4-6 (NLT). It's easy to allow frustration to take over when you see that child twirling in the back or listen to the chatter over the song, but I encourage you to take a breath, say a prayer, and allow God to work through you and into that child's life as they are in training to be a lifelong worshiper.

REPETITION! REPETITION! REPETITION!

It takes time to engage children in worship. I can't say that enough. Through your enthusiasm and example, you can train and lead the next generation into worship. If worship with children is something new to your ministry, take time to build a team that is passionate about leading children into authentic worship and then just start doing it. Keep doing it week after week. You will see progress made and lives changed as they connect with our Savior through worship.

Emily Hill is the Children's Ministry Director at New Stanton Church in PA. She is a trained social worker with a heart for reaching families throughout the local community. When she's not doing that, you can usually find her scrapbooking and binge-watching reality TV.

chapter 6

YOU CAN DANCE IF YOU WANT TO

Engaging Kids in Worship

BY AMBER KREIDER

IT SEEMS EVERYWHERE I look, we're all having trouble getting kids engaged in what we're doing. We're looking around at kids of all ages, backgrounds, and learning styles who are not "getting it." One area where I hear leaders complain about this happening, over and over, is during our worship times.

You spend an exorbitant amount of time searching, googling, downloading, and listening to music hoping to find THE song. You know the one. The one that will keep your preschoolers still, your third graders scream singing, and your fifth graders dancing. I haven't been in ministry as long as some of you seasoned saints out there, but I have learned pretty quickly, that song does not exist. So how, how in the world do you make sure the little lambs in your care are able to actively worship our great big God with all their hearts?

Check What You Expect. What does it look like when a kid is engaged in worship? You probably have an image in your mind, and it's probably a little different for each of us. For me, it's my 8-year-old, standing on a pew next to me in "Big Church" singing at the top of her lungs. My eyes got a little sweaty listening to her slightly off-key voice singing along with a room full of grown-ups. However, some weeks she sits cross-legged on the pew, with a clipboard on her lap, coloring pictures of unicorns during all of worship. Looking over at her, she looks completely unengaged in anything except what color to make the unicorn's horn. But if you sit very close, and listen very carefully, you'll hear her singing along. Without ever looking at the screen, she will quietly sing along, and more importantly, be able to tell you later what we sang about. When you look out at your kids during a worship set, remember that kids all interact with the world around them a little differently than the kid next to them. And each kid interacts differently on different days. Make sure your expectations are not unrealistic for your kids.

Make Sure They Understand. I worked for several years with a teen camp in northern Indiana. I didn't work much with teens outside of this, and my area was more administrative than hands-on. I remember in planning meetings, going over the schedule and people saying, "When should we have them do TAWG?" "Let's schedule TAWG for right after breakfast." "Should we program TAWG or let them do it alone?" I was new, and young, so it took me way longer than it should (maybe months) to say, "What is TAUG and why is everyone saying it like it's a normal word I should know?" I was then kindly informed that it stood for "Time Alone With God'" and was a phrase commonly used in the youth ministry community. To this day, every time I hear youth pastors use it, I kindly remind them that anyone who does not spend a ton of time in youth groups has no idea what they mean.

Don't let worship be "TAWG." While worship is a real word at least, don't let it be one of those things kids hear said a lot, but have no idea what it means. If you want kids to really get into worship, first they have to get it. This might be as simple as having a quick explanation before each set. It might be a more in-depth study of different biblical examples of scripture. Use whatever works best for your kids and culture. But make sure they know what it means. You must do all you can to assure that your kids don't graduate to youth group thinking worship is just singing Christian songs. They've got to understand!

Intergenerational Worship: Make Space for Chaos. If there's anything I would tell other churches they must do, it's make space for kids in "big" church. Didn't Jesus welcome the little children to Him? He pulled them, in all their chaos and craziness, onto His lap. Our churches must do the same. If you spend all your time separate, it will be difficult, if not impossible, for your children to acclimate to "big" church when they grow out of children's and youth ministries. This looks differently for each group of people in each church. For some it may be all the kids being in worship, and given space to dance, and ribbons and shaker eggs to help them worship. For others, it may be Fifth Sunday family services, which are wholly designed to minister to kids of all ages. For my church, it's occasional family services, and always having kindergarten-fifth graders join during our worship set in "big" church before they go to class. Whatever works for your church, just make sure there is a space for them beside the grown-ups. And that space needs to allow for them to be children. God created kids to wiggle, and wonder, and dance. If you try to stop them from doing any of that as they worship, what are you teaching them about worship?

Now you've laid your foundations. You're ready to expect all things, you've figured out how to teach kids what worship is, and you've made space for intergeneration worship. Now comes the actual worshipping through music part. There are three things I believe we all need to be sure are included in our worship ministries.

1. QUALITY

I remember seeing *The Little Mermaid* in theatres. It was epic! It felt like I was under water, right next to Ariel singing about how she loved a man she just saw one time on a boat. (Seriously Ariel? Get a grip girl! You could run a kingdom! Don't throw that away for some guy with good hair!) We, of course, owned the movie on VHS, and I watched it over and over as a child. Recently, I pulled out the movie to show my kids. It took some time to dig out a VCR and hook it up to the 60" HDTV at my parent's house, but we did it! After about three minutes, I couldn't even pay attention, because the quality of the picture was so terrible. It was amazing to see the advancements we've made in children's movies in the past 30 years!

I think we often try to put our "VHS" songs to our kids' "HDTV" brains and are confused why they don't get into it. Good, bad, or otherwise, we are surrounded by amazing technology. The kids don't know what a skipping CD sounds like, let alone a scratched record. Music in all other areas of their lives is presented to them in crisp clear digital. Even the background music on their YouTube videos is high quality music. If you're trying to use the same CD, or videos your church has used the past 30 years ... don't. That sounds so harsh, and I thought about trying to put it more delicately, but there it is. This doesn't mean that old songs are not worthwhile any more; I just encourage you to update how you present them. Think about how the worship team prepares for the adults at your church. It's common for worship teams to practice ahead of time, carefully pick out songs, audition musicians, and continually update their database of songs. Aren't our kids worth some effort too? One of the beautiful things about drowning in information and technology is that you have access to so much great stuff. You are no stranger to working within a budget and limited resources. Don't let that stop you from giving your kids a quality worship experience. Maybe you carefully select some great musicians to play live. Maybe you invest some money in a better sound system for your kids. Whatever you do, give your kids the highest quality worship experience you can, because it will help them focus better, just as it would an adult.

2. VARIETY

I think one of the easiest ways to get your kids engaged in worship is to offer up as much variety as possible. Let them experience different styles, atmospheres, and music. Some kids will engage best right alongside a parent. Some will be able to worship best while doing crazy motions. Some do better with live music, some better with video, some with CD. Mix it up! Offer different experiences occasionally (or regularly if possible). Not only will you engage different kids, in different ways, it also helps teach kids that worship is not just one thing. Worship is not just a guy behind a piano with low lights. It's not just when everyone is singing loud and people are dancing in the aisle. It's all these things and more. I told you at the beginning of the chapter that there is no one song that is perfect, and there is no one style that is perfect either.

3. TRUTH

When you ask a kid what they learned at school or church, if the answer isn't "Nothing" or "I don't know" it's likely not more than a single sentence. No matter how great the lesson was, or beautiful the music was, kids will often walk away with one nugget of truth. We've learned this often in our teaching. Most curriculums have one driving point that everything centers around, knowing if kids only walk away remembering one thing, they hope it's this. Have you thought about that in the worship songs you pick? If your kid only absorbs a little bit of that song, will it be one full of truth and depth? Or will it be the part that says "Nah, Nah, Nah" or "Yeah, Yeah, Yeah, Jesus" over and over? Sometimes you pick a song just because it's something kids will sing along and dance to. But I would challenge you to find ones that are both full of truth and depth with a great beat. Charles Spurgeon writes in *Come Ye Children*: "Teach the little ones the whole truth and nothing but the truth; for instruction is the great want of the child's nature. A child has not only to live as you and I have, but also to grow; hence he has double need of food." Use your worship time to give them whole truth, and double portions!

4. MUSIC IS POWERFUL.

You use it to memorize things; it calms you and gives you energy; it helps you remember and express yourself. There is a reason the church historically uses music as a main tool for worship. Be careful how you use this tool, though! If your kids are humming a song all week, do all you can to be sure it's one full of deep spiritual truth. Children seem to always understand more than you think. Don't be afraid to use songs you think might be "over their heads." It might be for now, but music has a way of burying deep within you, waiting to come out when ou need it most. You know there's that one karaoke song that you forgot you knew, but when your friends are all singing it, you somehow remember all the words. Use that tool to plant seeds of solid doctrine in our kids.

5. ADULTS

Finally, the most important part of kids engaging in anything is the adults around them. Make sure the grown-ups who are pouring into the kids they work with are engaging in the worship time. I always tell my volunteers, kids will show about 50% of the energy you show. If your worship time involves doing motions, and all the volunteers stand at the back, kids will not engage as well. If your leader just stands on the stage and sings one song after another until the list of songs is finished, your kids will do the same. You must model for your kids what worship looks like—in service and out of it. Challenge your volunteers to learn the songs, to study the lyrics, to worship right alongside the kids. There will always be a kid poking the kid next to her, or whispering to his neighbor. Don't focus on them unless you really have to. Focus on worshiping our great big God, who loves hearing you sing, loud or quiet, dancing or still, with a piano or video. He is so good and so worthy of all of it!

Amber Kreider is the Children's Ministry Director at a neighborhood church in South Bend, IN. She loves being able to wear novelty T-shirts to work and getting the pastors to dress up in costume. It's her desire to create a space for kids to learn to love Jesus and the local church, all while embracing the abundance of whimsy and joy that God intentionally created in them. She also loves coffee, sci-fi, and filling her bike basket with snacks and riding around the neighborhood.

chapter 7

ONCE UPON A YESTERDAY

Engaging Kids Through Storytelling

BY TAMMY JONES

W HO DOESN'T LOVE a good story? I know I do! You most likely do too. Even if you don't, you're still interacting with stories every day. Books, movies, television, social media, or even a simple conversation with a friend are all stories of one kind or another. It's amazing what some people can convey in 280 characters!

People were sharing stories long before any written word came along. Storytelling was the most effective way to share family history or other important information people didn't want forgotten. Storytelling was the method used by parents in the Bible to teach children about God. *"These words that I am giving you today are to be in your heart. Repeat them to your children. Talk about them when you sit in your house and when you walk along the road, when you lie down and when you get up"* Deuteronomy 6:6-7 (CSB). Parents are commanded to share God's story with their children orally! Those in children's ministry should be using the same method to engage the kids in their ministries.

Although kids are saturated with videos and high-tech genius graphics, you can still get most kids to fully engage with a good story ... that is if the story is told well. An engaging story must be told with plenty of action, using expressions of the face, movement of the body, inflection of the voice, and plenty of dazzling action words. The sharing of the story must be practiced beforehand to nail down the timing and delivery. Your stories should be relatable and include ways that the children can participate in it. Props, sound effects, and costumes can be used to catch and keep the attention of kids. When all these elements are in place, even the most avid YouTube fan will be on the edge of their seat and completely engrossed in your story!

I see what you're saying! Whether you're sharing a Bible story (read Bible narrative) or one that you have read or imagined, expression is very important. Facial expressions are your graphics! Over-exaggerate expressions to make them as big as possible. Make your eyes overly large with surprise. Make your smile from ear to ear with happiness. Make your eyebrows meet in the middle for a really angry face. (Don't worry that you may look silly. It's okay. Really!)

Your body movements should be over the top as well. Let the children see the hugeness of Goliath and the small stature of Zacchaeus. Let them see how Saul must have looked when he fell on his knees on the Damascus road and hid his face. Show them how Mary looked when the angel announced that she would have a baby or her body racked with grief when Jesus was being crucified on the cross. Body movements help punctuate the story and keep it moving.

As you're telling the story, be sure to use words that will help create an image in the minds of the children. Use lots of action words and descriptive words. Along with your body movements and facial expressions, these words will begin forming images that the children will piece together to make a video in their minds. This will become invaluable for recall later on.

Costumes and props can also be invaluable tools to help create images for the children and keep them engaged in the story. These items need not be elaborate or expensive. In fact, the more simple the items are, the better. The more simple the items are then the more the children (and you) will have to tap into their imaginations. As you listen to them retell the story at a later time, you'll see that each child "saw" the story in a way unique to them.

You may even want to add in a few sound effects or at least some background noise to create an atmosphere. There are many free sound effects that are available online. Scents are helpful in creating an atmosphere also. Recently at our church, we created four escape rooms for our Easter event. Each room represented a different part of the Easter story. In the first room, we created a marketplace with fresh vegetables and other items for sale along with a booth, trees, and a donkey. In the second room we created the garden where Jesus was arrested. In that room were lots of trees and flowers. The third room was the palace where Pilate tried to free Jesus but the crowd chose Barabbas. The last room depicted the cross and tomb. Each room had its own sights, sounds, and smells to help create a realistic experience for families as they went through the rooms solving puzzles. We found air fresheners that really helped with the floral smells. We used a lavender scent for the cross and tomb in the last room as the atmosphere was reverent and quiet. However, we had a bit of difficulty finding a scent for the jail and sweaty prisoners for the palace room!

Practice makes perfect. Preparation is very important in storytelling. You take away from the story if you forget portions or repeat them. If you bomb the most exciting part of the story, well then, sorry, but you just blew the story and that's all they'll remember. You must memorize the story you have selected to tell. Here are a few tips that I picked up from a group called Simply the Story. This group trains people to use oral strategies to tell stories from the Bible for evangelistic purposes, especially in countries where Christians cannot share their faith openly.

Begin preparing by reading the Bible selection to yourself. Read the selection again out loud this time paying careful attention to action or descriptive words. Now try to repeat the story without looking back at the selection. Read the selection out loud again. Try to repeat the story for a second time from memory. Keep repeating this process until you have memorized the story with the details. I find it helpful to make mental markers by breaking down the story into three parts: beginning, middle, and end. Then, I try to visualize what happened in each part. This helps me remember the specific details for the sections. Mental markers are helpful for remembering names and details. For instance, make nonsense words or silly pictures to help you remember, such as picturing Zacchaeus as a tiny little man who wears a chain with a large Z around his neck and drags around a large key.

Now that you have the story memorized, it's time to practice telling the story out loud. Pay careful attention to the details of the story and use all the suggestions mentioned above. Practice until you can tell the story naturally. The story should flow from your lips without any hesitation or hiccups. It should feel like you've told it a thousand times even though you haven't.

Timing is another element of an engaging story. Think through the story, looking for the movement in it. Search specifically for places where the movement is slow or fast, intense or calm. Be sure to match your speech and movements to match with the natural flow of the story.

Participation ribbons for everyone. Be creative in finding ways to engage the kids with your story through physical activity or repetition of some kind. Have the kids clap a rhythm at certain points in the story or perhaps they could repeat certain responses when you cue them with special words. Ask the kids to join you in your movements as you tell the story. Have them walk on the water with Jesus, climb down the rope from Rahab's rooftop, or march around the walls of Jericho with Joshua. Don't you wave palm branches on Palm Sunday? Physical movements activate the children's ability to pay attention and thus gets and keeps them engaged with the story.

One of my favorite ways to actively involve children with a story is to have them retell it on their own using my props. They must tell the whole story in detail. There's a catch though. The children must use each prop while telling the story as quickly as possible. Fastest time wins! The kids love doing this and the stories can sometimes be hilarious. I find the Christmas story is one of the favorites in my class to do this with.

Another way to allow the children to participate in the story is to tell the story while doing a science experiment or a cooking demonstration or even crafting something. Provide enough supplies for the children to replicate the experiment after the demonstration. Help them make their own recipe along with you. Allow time for the children to make their own craft or art to take home while you demonstrate and tell the story. While they work ask the children to repeat the story as exactly as possible and to discuss and make applications to their lives.

I can relate. Please don't be offended, but sometimes children have a hard time relating to Bible stories. Yes, I know that we're supposed to teach life application and moral implications and the answer to "What has this got to do with me?" questions. That is all well and good and useful and the right thing to do. However, if you start out with something that the kids can relate to, then you're already ahead of the game.

I like to find or make up my own stories based on biblical ones but include elements of life that the kids see and interact with on a daily basis. After telling this story, I move on to tell the Bible story and even have the kids read along in their Bibles. We have had some great discussion times. Kids have been amazed that the Bible actually spoke to things that they were going through right now at home or school. Making the stories more relatable in this way is not changing the story or making less of the Bible; it is simply using another story to help the children see what was there all along. The children learn to look below the surface of the story, past the simple moral applications to see the character of God—who He is, what He's like, and how much He cares about the details of their lives. All this from a simple story? Yes! When you make the Bible relatable the children will stay engaged.

A word of caution. When you make your stories interesting and the children are completely immersed, hanging on your every word, be careful. It's possible to make the contemporary stories a bit too memorable. I was teaching on the prodigal son one Sunday morning. I decided to first tell a story about a man who made a living driving a garbage truck and then relate the story to the biblical prodigal son. Well, the kids loved the story and we had a really good time discussing all the ins and outs of what happened. They wondered why the son ran away and why he was afraid to come home. They wanted to understand why the father reacted the way he did, welcoming his son home with open arms instead of chastising him for running away. It was a great day! I felt so good about what we had accomplished that morning that I confidently asked one of my students to tell their parents about what we had learned in class. The boy repeated to his mother the entire contemporary story that I had told that morning. Then I asked him to please tell his mother what else we had learned in class. He could not remember anything else from that morning's lesson. Be careful people.

Storytelling is the simplest (and most fun) way to engage kids with your subject matter. It lends itself to all kinds of topics. Just be sure to use expression, props, participation, and practice, practice, practice—unless boring was what you were going for.

Tammy Jones is the Children's Minister at Cove Creek Baptist Church. There's nothing she won't do for kids. Her pastor says he never knows what she may drag down the hallway past his office.

chapter 8

DON'T WORRY, I SAW THIS ON MACGYVER

Engaging Kids with Object Lessons and Props

BY AARON LABARGE

PAPER CLIPS AND DUCT TAPE were MacGyvers' go to tools. He could save the world with just those few things and a little creativity. However, you are not MacGyver. Nevertheless, you can learn something from this show. Imagination and ingenuity! It's what made the show so great. Those two things can have the same impact in ministering to kids.

"Imagination is the most important thing the human mind has." – MacGyver

Object lessons give us a chance to teach in ways that implement imagination in learning. They allow kids and even adults to learn in a way that entices their minds. If you've ever sat through a boring lecture where someone just read from notes, you probably can't remember much of what was taught. However, if they had walked in and given the presentation wearing a Batman mask holding an umbrella, I bet you would struggle to forget it. Not only would you struggle to forget it, you'd probably go and talk about it with others. That's what object lessons can do for ministry teaching.

The great thing is we don't have to be MacGyver to come up with a good object lesson. Most of the time it's simply looking at what we want to teach and imagining how to do so. Creativity and ingenuity can handle the rest.

THE OBJECTLESS OBJECT LESSON

Talk about keeping it simple, I once did an object lesson with no object. I talked about being prepared when our time comes. I acted distraught like I couldn't figure out what I was supposed to be doing. Finally, I just said, "I guess I'm just not prepared today." They remember that lesson. They talked about it for a couple of weeks. They laughed as they picked on me for not being prepared. Nevertheless, they remembered the lesson and that is the key. If you can find a way that helps kids remember then you're on to something.

There are a lot of resources out there to help us. I think none are greater than your own mind and the Bible. But, if you do struggle with finding ideas, I'll be honest, I watch videos teaching me magic tricks, read articles on how to make slime, and purchase books by awesome leaders like Tina Houser, to get ideas. Yet some of the greatest ideas still come from me looking around at what I have and connecting the dots.

I could even sit here and give you a hundred ideas for object lessons. But, as the old saying goes, "Give a man a fish and feed him for a day. Teach a man to fish and feed him for a lifetime." My hope is after reading this that you not only see the significance of object and propped based lessons, but that you have the capability to do them on your own as well.

JESUS AND FEET

Did you know Jesus Himself used object lessons for teaching? In John 13:3-17 (NASB) He washed the disciples' feet to teach them about being servants. *"For I gave you an example that you also should do as I did to you. Truly, truly, I say to you, a slave is not greater than his master, nor is one who is sent greater than the one who sent him. If you know these things, you are blessed if you do them."*

Jesus used this technique to make it real for the disciples. There are some key examples you can take away from His teaching when you do object lessons.

JESUS MADE IT REAL.

Jesus could have simply explained or talked about Him washing their feet. Instead, He did it. Scripture says *"Then He poured water into the basin, and began to wash the disciples' feet and to wipe them with the towel with which He was girded"* John 13:5 (NASB). He got His hands dirty by actively taking them through the process. This is the heart of presenting an object lesson—to give a physical representation. I can tell you about the size of the Grand Canyon or I can take you there. Which would be more impactful? Hearing is only one sense; yet, a good object lesson uses multiple, if not all the senses. By enticing all the senses, we can imprint the event onto someone's brain.

"The sense of smell is closely linked with memory, probably more so than any of our other senses." ("Fifth Sense, creativityforhire.co.uk)

JESUS MADE IT RELATABLE.

Jesus took something they understood and used it. The washing of feet would've been a common practice in those days since people walked most places. If hearers cannot relate to the lesson, they probably won't pay attention. Making it relatable often makes it easier to understand.

JESUS STARTED WITH PETER.

By starting with Peter, Jesus was able to get an active response. Peter was always the one blurting something out. This makes him a great person to use, because he will be an active participant. Sometimes, having a child with you asking questions and being curious helps push the message along. They're great at helping to present ideas from the child's perspective. Having that one child be first also helps, because he will ask many of the questions that the others are thinking.

JESUS KEPT CONTROL.

Even though Jesus started with Peter, letting him ask questions, Jesus still guided the message to where He desired it to go. By telling Peter that he will understand afterwards, Jesus created an environment where He did not lose control. He created anticipation for the answer that was to come.

Make it real, make it relatable, involve others when possible, and keep control. To me this is what makes a perfect object lesson. Kids are naturally curious. You know this by interacting with them. Object lessons help you tap into that curiosity. Then you use that curiosity and their senses to help them both understand and remember what is being taught.

BANANAS AND TUNA FISH

I hope when you think of bananas and tuna fish you realize they have nothing in common. The biggest issue in using object lessons is often you try too hard to connect things that have no business being connected. There are many good ideas out there but not every idea is a good idea. So often in an effort to be inventive, people find something cool and then try to make it work with whatever they're teaching at the time. You are basically trying to make a square peg fit into a triangular hole. It does not work. You can't just force things to work.

Let me better explain myself with this example. Recently, I saw a post on social media from a youth pastor who bought a 12-foot beach ball. His comment above the picture of the massive beach ball was "just bought this, any ideas?" There's an issue if he tries to take this beach ball and make it fit into whatever he is teaching at the time. Moving forward with the example, let's say he is currently teaching on the plagues of Egypt. A 12-foot beach ball probably is not going to work best when teaching this. Does that mean it is useless in teaching? No. It's just not the right place.

This is where you truly can become dynamic in using object lessons or props. This awesome item can be set aside and brought out for a different lesson. You can use it as the earth in the creation story. You can use it in a size comparison in the story of David and Goliath. A good object lesson is defined by its ability to add to the lesson, not by its ability to entertain or confuse.

NOT CREATIVE?

I know you may have read through here and thought, "I can't do this. I'm not creative." Personally, I believe having the ability to create is in us all. Being image bearers of God we all have the ability to create. Nevertheless, I understand for some it comes very naturally. Moreover, for others it is like trying to give a cat a bath (a pain-filled experience).

What I say to those who struggle is it's okay to use resources. When I decided I needed transportation to work, I didn't go out and try to build a car. That would have been ridiculous, plus who has time to build a car from scratch? Not me. Instead, I researched vehicles based on my need. In addition, in today's world there is so much available right at your fingertips: Youtube, Pinterest, Facebook groups, kidmin idea books, and I've even found podcasts that present ideas.

The key is if you struggle to find ideas, don't be afraid of researching resources. You can easily beat yourself up thinking, "I have to do it all. It has to be from my brain and nowhere else; otherwise, it's not genuine ministry." Your heart for God is what makes it genuine, not that you made it up. If you're just looking for stuff so you don't have to come up with anything, then your heart isn't in it. Now you're not being genuine.

CONCLUSION

There are many great resources out there to help with ideas for object or prop based lessons. There are many ways to go about creating your own lessons. However, no matter the resource or the object used, if you aren't connecting to God's Word on a regular basis, it will reflect in your teaching. So study God's Word first, and always make it the foundation of the lesson.

Aaron LaBarge is currently serving as the Student and Family Pastor at a church in Columbia, KY. He is a father, husband, former Army soldier of 8+ years, pastor, kid with ADHD, student, friend, and most importantly, Christian who seeks to honor God through everything he does. He likes to think he has a somewhat different perspective on ministry due to his unique journey in life.

chapter 9

THINKING BEYOND THE BOOK

Engaging Kids in Bible Reading

BY ANDREW WOUTERS

"So faith comes from hearing, and hearing through the word of Christ" Romans 10:17 (ESV).

BOOKS HAVE BEEN ENGAGING and captivating adults and kids for centuries. If this is the case, then why is it so difficult for you to engage kids today in reading the Bible? If your kids grow up not wanting to engage themselves in the Bible, then it will be very hard for there to be faith formation in their lives. We know that very clearly from Romans 10:17.

Growing up I wasn't very interested in reading books. Movies, documentaries, and television shows were my preferred method of information gathering and entertainment. As I grew older, I noticed that when I read for information and for the entertainment it was more impressed upon me. The Bible has the ability to do the same thing. *"For the word of God is living and active, sharper than any two-edged sword, piercing to the division of soul and spirit, of joints and marrow, and discerning the thoughts and intentions of the heart"* Hebrews 4:12 (ESV). The Bible is not just any book. The Bible is living and active and it has the ability to pierce the soul and spirit. That's why it's so important that you engage kids in reading God's Word at church and working with parents to continue that at home. I believe when you do that, these kids will form a faith that will last a lifetime.

I want to share with you 9 practical keys to engaging kids in reading their Bible in church and at home.

1. IT'S A STORY. TREAT IT LIKE ONE.

The Bible is not just a book of history but a book full of captivating stories. I've never met a kid who came home from school wanting to read their history book. I know I wasn't one. So why would you treat the Bible as only a historical book. When Jesus taught, He didn't stand up there and just give the facts about what needed to be done. He shared stories with the people that they would understand and relate to. When I read those stories, I can imagine the fluctuation in Jesus' voice as He told the parable of the mustard seed, *"He said therefore, What is the kingdom of God like? And to what shall I compare it? It is like a grain of mustard seed that a man took and sowed in his garden, and it grew and became a tree, and the birds of the air made nests in its branches"* Luke 13:18-19 (ESV).

Now I want you to read those two verses again. Think about how you can tell a story while reading it. The Bible is more than words and sentences. You want the kids to be immersed in the story. Help them do that.

2. MAKE BIBLE READING FUN!

Kids tend to be more likely to engage when they're having fun. One thing we enjoy doing while reading the Bible in our elementary service is to act it out. I'm not talking about something rehearsed with adults or even youth helpers. I'm talking about picking out a few kids to act out the story as you read it. When kids are up and engaged in the story through acting, they're having to comprehend what they're hearing. This is a storytelling method we use in our own home with our four girls. Our older two love to act out the story and dress up like the characters.

One other activity we enjoy doing is have the kids read a passage of scripture alone or in teams. After they've done that, we have pictures that portray what they just read. The pictures are not displayed in order. Their job is to put the pictures in order and tell the story back to us. This is a fun way they engage with the Bible. It's also reproducible for at home.

3. APPLY IT TO WHERE THEY ARE AND WHAT THEY'RE DOING.

One series of books I remember reading as I was growing up was *The Chronicles of Narnia*. When I read this series, I always imagined myself in the awesome world of Narnia that C.S. Lewis created. I always asked myself, "What if I lived in Narnia?"

The Bible is more engaging to kids when they see themselves in it. When I read a passage of scripture, I always ask myself, "How does this apply to me?" I also challenge our kids to ask the same question. When a child can make a personal connection with what they are reading, it will stick with them.

One question I always get from students is, "That's a cool story, but I'm going through this or that. How can this story help me?" That's a real question you hear all too often and how you answer it is the difference between an engaged child and a disengaged child. You might not have the answer right at that moment, but you can help them find the answer. You can do that by either seeking wisdom and counsel or by turning to scripture. Remember when a child asks that kind of question, they are engaging in what they are reading and they are seeking to sharpen themselves. *"Iron sharpens iron, and one man sharpens another"* Proverbs 27:17 (ESV).

4. ALLOW THE KIDS TO READ THE SCRIPTURES.

You're reading point number four and thinking, "DUH!" I'm not talking about on their own or even just in small groups. I mean, let them read during the lesson or storytelling time. First of all, you should make every effort to ensure that each kid has a Bible while you are teaching and reading it. How can a child engage in something that they themselves are not holding in their hands. This is similar to me asking my daughter to play with a toy, but the toy is hidden in the closet.

When I storytell, I rarely read the scriptures myself. I've noticed that the kids engage more with what they are reading when they do. By allowing the children to do this it gets them into the habit of reading the Bible. They learn that reading the Bible isn't hard. It's just like reading any other book.

5. ALLOW FOR DISCUSSION AS YOU TEACH THE WORD.

"All Scripture is breathed out by God and profitable for teaching, for reproof, for correction, and for training in righteousness, that the man of God may be complete, equipped for every good work" 2 Timothy 3:16-17 (ESV).

I've used discussion as an important part of our teaching time for two years now and have noticed several benefits when it comes to engaging kids in reading the Word. First, I can tell who has been paying attention and who has been reading at home. One of the most important parts of what we do is challenge students to read the passage of scripture for the following week's lesson during the week before. Second, when we allow a platform for kids to ask questions about what they are learning, they engage more often. Third, discussion is a critical part of the learning process. Not only does it allow the students to discuss their thoughts with their leaders, but it challenges them to listen and respond to their peers.

6. UTILIZE A VERSION OF THE BIBLE THEY CAN UNDERSTAND.

I have nothing against the King James Version of the Bible, but I don't find it to be very helpful in getting kids to engage in the Bible. Kids need something they can understand. They need something that is written in language they use. There are many versions out there that accomplish this. I challenge you to read them and decide for yourself. We use the NIV when we teach in our elementary service and the NIrV in our toddler service.

7. RESOURCE YOUR KIDS AND PARENTS.

The parents and kids at your church don't know everything that is available to them, like you might. They might be looking for a good kid-friendly study Bible to kick-start reading at home. Help resource them with that. I learned very early on in ministry that I need the help of parents. Kids are only in our care at most twice a week for a couple of hours. They are at home every day for much longer than a couple of hours. Not only do we provide extended resources for our parents, but we send home the afore-mentioned pre-teach sheet with our families every weekend. This pre-teach sheet allows the parents or guardians to intro-duce the lesson to their kids and lead them in the Bible reading for the weekend.

Make sure you're familiar with the resource before you rec-ommend it. You want to be ready and available for questions whenever they come.

8. CHALLENGE THE KIDS TO READ GOD'S WORD.

You cannot engage in something that you're not reading. One of the ways I use to get kids to read their Bibles is to issue a challenge. Kids love to earn things and they love competition. We challenge the kids to read a specific amount of scripture in a specific amount of time. When they do so, they get their name entered into a drawing to win a prize every so often.

We utilize a program called JBQ which challenges kids to learn scripture. You can learn more about JBQ at *kidmin. ag.org/ministries/juniorbiblequiz/overview.* We also use *Hiding the Word in My Heart* by Tina Houser. We love the fun and engaging ways she provides for kids to learn scripture.

9. KEEP THEM ACCOUNTABLE.

When setting up a new habit in anyone's life, accountability is a must. Someone there to keep them accountable and see how they are doing will definitely help them succeed. Keep the kids accountable in their Bible reading challenges. Don't have the "set it and forget it" mindset.

At home I don't tell my 3-year-old daughter to go clean her room and expect her to do it without having to check up on her. I have to constantly be watching over her to make sure she completes the task. The same accountability will apply when she begins to read her Bible on her own. We keep them accountable because we love them and want to see them reach eternity.

Engaging kids in reading God's Word is definitely no easy task with today's generation, but it is a task that can change the course of their eternity. I believe these nine practical keys will help you both in kids' service and at home to engage your kids in reading the most important book of all. *"So faith comes from hearing, and hearing through the word of Christ"* Romans 10:17 (ESV).

I challenge you to treat it like a story, make it fun, give application, let them read during service, discuss, make it understandable, resource kids and parents, set forth challenges for your kids, and most importantly, keep them accountable.

Andrew Wouters has a wife, Terra, and 4 wonderful girls: Dallas, Phoenix, Shiloh, and Everest. When he's not doing kids' ministry, he enjoys puppets, BBQ, and coffee.

chapter 10

SMALL BUT MIGHTY

Engaging Kids with the Practice of Prayer

BY JOY FEEMSTER

GOD IS GREAT, God is good. Let us thank Him for our food." "Now I lay me down to sleep, I pray the Lord my soul to keep." The prayers of children are often seen as rote, simplistic, and mostly a tool to teach them to pray.

However, in the same way that there is no junior Holy Spirit, there's also no pee-wee prayers. If you realize that kids have the same Holy Spirit residing in them and helping them pray, the same Jesus in heaven interceding for and with them as they pray, and the same Father God who hears their every word, how would that change the way you think of children's prayers?

Our kids have the potential to be powerful prayer warriors—small, but mighty!

But how do you get from the early childhood rote, sing-song prayers (which are appropriate for those years) and the "bless my puppy" prayers (he died two years ago, by the way, but we've prayed for that puppy in Sunday school ever since), to prayers with meaning and power?

To begin with, I've noticed that kids are not always clearly taught about what prayer is and is not. They need to know that prayer is not just a bunch of words. *"And when you pray, do not keep on babbling like pagans, for they think they will be heard for their many words"* Matthew 6:7 (NIV). Kids need to know that prayer is conversation with God. I've made the mistake of saying that prayer is talking to God, but that's only partly right. Prayer is a two-way dialogue with God. He is always listening when you speak, but you need to make sure to speak and then listen for what God is saying. Many children think prayer is what they say, but have no idea that God would actually speak to them! Teaching kids to hear His voice through His Word and impressions given by the Holy Spirit is incredibly important. It's a huge step in having a real relationship with God.

Children also need to understand the importance of prayer. Show them that the Bible tells you that you are to *"pray continually"* 1 Thessalonians 5:17 (NIV). It also shows you that God hears your prayers about everything in your life, big or small, *"... in every situation, by prayer and petition, with thanksgiving, present your requests to God"* Philippians 4:6 (NIV). It teaches that you have the power to intercede for others in prayer, *"... pray for each other that you may be healed. The prayer of a righteous person is powerful and effective"* James 5:16 (NIV).

In this day and time, many parents have either abdicated the role of spiritual training in their households, or do not even know how to pray themselves. Having their kids modeling prayer for them and praying for them has the potential to change lives in the whole family! Also, how easy it is for kids to have the opportunity to pray with and for their friends at school, at soccer or dance practice, and other places where, as an adult, you have no entrée.

Showing kids, then, that they have been put where they are *"for such a time as this"* Esther 4:14 (NIV) can help them see the importance of prayer and help motivate them to intercede for their schools, their friends, and their families. When kids get hold of the idea that they can really make a difference in their world, they get excited!

So how do you lead kids to have their own real and meaningful prayer lives? Well, they don't call it the "practice of prayer" for nothing! Kids need to learn how to pray, and to practice praying regularly until it becomes as natural as breathing. Obviously, this takes time and continual instruction. Mostly, it takes prayer on your part for wisdom and direction from God, to help your little friends learn to pray. As children's pastors, children's ministry workers, or volunteers, it is imperative that you show the kids under your care that prayer is the real deal. It's your communication with your great God. They can make a difference in the world through your sincere prayers. You have to keep *"asking, seeking, and knocking"* Matthew 7:7-8 (NIV).

Begin by modeling prayer to them. You pray, they listen. You talk about things in their lives that need prayer, then you give them the opportunity to pray about them. Sometimes, you get the "puppy prayers." Other times, you get fervent prayers about their life situations, such as the time one of our kids prayed for her dad who was homeless. She prayed for his health and safety. She prayed for him to find a job. She prayed for him to make better choices so he could have a home. All of this from a child of five years old!

Here are some practical ways to help kids learn to pray or deepen their prayer life.

Practice prayer together. Go around the circle, each praying for their own needs, then as they become more used to it, go around and have them pray for one another's needs. You can have them gather around each person as they are being prayed for, put their hands on the child's shoulders or arms (if the child is willing). If you really want to be surprised at children's prayers, gather them around and pray for YOU! Keep the tissue box handy!

Practice prayer on their own. The children can simply turn around and face away from the group, eyes closed, and pray to themselves, or you can direct them to their specific separate places in the room where they can pray on their own. If you choose to do this, a great help is to lower the lighting a bit and play some reflective music. In fact, I would recommend doing this whenever they are praying, as it gives them a signal that you are doing something different now, something special. Jumpstart3 has some music called "Altar the Atmosphere", created especially for times like these. After prayer time, ask, "Did you feel that God was saying something to you?" "If so, what was it?" Write these things down for the younger ones. For the older ones, encourage them to journal these God moments so they can look back at them frequently.

Older kids can model prayer to younger ones which is a helpful practice to both. Kids can have a prayer buddy who prays with and for them, and who also challenges them to think of others they could be praying with and for.

Practice different positions for prayer. We don't want kids to think they can only pray at certain times and places with heads bowed and eyes closed. Prayer can be any way that helps you talk to or listen to God. Prayer can be in the moment, such as Nehemiah's "arrow prayer" (Nehemiah 2:4-5). Prayer position can be a response to what is being prayed about, such as when Ezra wrote in Ezra 9:5-6 (NIV) *"(I) ... fell on my hands and knees with my hands spread out to the Lord God and prayed: 'O my God, I am too ashamed and disgraced to lift my face up to you, my God, because our sins are higher than our heads and our guilt has reached the heavens."* Or when, in 2 Samuel 12, David lay prostrate, praying for his infant son's life. Allow kids the opportunity to practice praying while standing, kneeling, sitting, or lying down. Let them pray with hands raised or outstretched, with eyes open or closed, praying in silence, praying out loud, or praying in song. Let them see that God hears them all the time. You can pray every way, every day.

Incorporate prayer stations. I am a big fan of prayer stations, because I've seen them be very effective with older and younger children, teens and even adults. They are especially good for kids who need a focus or who are fidgety, as it gives them something concrete to do. Prayer stations can be very simple or quite elaborate, depending on your time and resources. I've used them in a simple way in my class each week, but then much more elaborately for prayer events that we have done.

There are many, many ideas for prayer stations on Pinterest. I have a Pinterest Board called Prayer Stations and Activities, where I have gathered a boatload of ideas together. The link for it is *https://pin.it6icsbh3fi6xgwu.* Most of these ideas require very few materials, such as Blessing Blocks, where you stack blocks or Legos, and thank God for something He has blessed you with as you stack each block. Or the Healing Board, where you write the names of someone who is sick or injured on a Band Aid and pray over it as you place it onto a poster board. One of my favorite prayer stations is called At the Cross. Draw a large cross onto poster board. Sit a container of black rocks on one side, and a container of clear stones on the other. Each child takes a black rock in their hand and while holding it, reflects on their sins that Jesus died for on the cross. Then they pray, asking for forgiveness for those sins. Next, they place the black rock on the cross, and take a clear stone with them, to remind them that Jesus has washed their sins away. You can place prayer stations in each corner of the room and have a certain amount of time for them during Sunday school, or other times you meet with your kids. You can even go outside and observe the beauty of nature, and give thanks for God's creation. That's always an amazing prayer station! Having a whole class period, or a longer special time to do more prayer stations is a great way to emphasize and practice prayer. Kids really engage with these, and surprisingly, teens and adults love them, too!

Teach Bible stories that show great moments in prayer. King Jehoshaphat prayed when faced with an overwhelming army arrayed against God's people. *"For we have no power to face this vast army that is attacking us. We do not know what to do, but our eyes are on you"* 2 Chronicles 20:12 (NIV). Remember Hannah when she dedicated Samuel to the temple, *"I prayed for this child, and the Lord granted me what I asked of Him"* 1 Samuel 1:27 (NIV), or when Esther had all the Jews in the capital pray with her before she went in to see the king to try to save her people from extermination (Esther 4:15-17) You could do a whole series of how the prayers of God's people brought about miracles though His power! Then make it real to the kids, and gather stories from people they know in your church or community who have testimonies of the power of prayer. You could bring in a special guest to talk about their experience. Don't forget to ask the kids about their prayer experiences!

God is not a gumball machine. On the flip side, you must be careful to help children see that God is not a giant bubble gum machine—in goes the prayer, out comes the favorable result. What happens when their prayers aren't answered in the way they expect, when it doesn't look like it was answered at all, or when God says "no"? You must let them know that God is sovereign, meaning He rules and reigns and always knows what's best, even if it doesn't look like the best thing to us. Also, you have to show them that God answers in His own perfect timing, not on your schedule. Sometimes, what looks like a "no", is just a "wait," and sometimes God just says "no." It is very helpful for kids to keep a record of their prayers and the answers to them. They can use notebook journals, or there are quite a few apps that will allow you to post your prayer requests and the answers to them in an ongoing electronic prayer journal. Seeing the answers to prayers as they come helps build their faith and motivates them to pray more.

What did Jesus say? Of course, any discussion on prayer should ask what Jesus had to say about it! He taught His disciples to pray, in what we know as the Lord's Prayer (Luke 11:1-4, Matthew 6:9-15). You should teach your kids these same principles: adoration of God, submission to His will, requests for your daily needs, forgiveness of your sins, protection, and guidance when tempted. There are many good teaching books available on the Lord's Prayer for kids. Every child should learn this prayer, not just as a rote memorization, but as a template to use in their own prayers.

All right, now—it's time to get on your knees and pray! Pray for the children under your sphere of influence. Pray for them to be open to the promptings of the Holy Spirit as you teach them to pray. Pray for His guidance and direction as you put together your lessons and as you teach. I'll be praying for each one who reads this chapter, and for those children under your care. *"May the grace of the Lord Jesus Christ, and the love of God, and the fellowship of the Holy Spirit be with you all"* 2 Corinthians 13:14 (NIV).

Joy Feemster is a 20-year veteran of children's ministry, who lives in South Carolina with her husband, 2 teens, dogs, cats, and a guinea pig. Her greatest fear is a worldwide coffee shortage.

chapter 11

WRITE IT DOWN
Engaging Kids Through Journaling

BY TINA HOUSER

IN RECENT YEARS, school systems have put a huge emphasis on kids participating in regular journaling exercises. This is a great plus for the community of faith as we encourage kids to make spiritual journaling part of their personal disciplines. Just as individuals have preferences on hairstyles, clothing styles, the sports they play, and a plethora of other partialities they have, the actual form that journaling takes is specific to the person doing it.

First of all, let's just clarify what journaling, as a spiritual discipline, is. Journaling is when a person makes a record of something. That's where the similarities end, because from there, what is recorded, how it's recorded, and how much is recorded reflects the journalist's personality, spiritual maturity, and pathway strengths they prefer to use in processing information. Spiritual journaling is a way of carrying on a conversation with the Lord through the written word. The person journaling is just using a different medium that requires him to slow down and share thoughts that are more intentional and thought out.

The Bible is a collection of journaling. The Letters of Paul are full of descriptions of what is going on, his thoughts, and how he thinks certain issues should be resolved. David gives us insight into his personal spiritual journal through the Psalms—a poetic and musical journal. Matthew, Mark, Luke and John journal about many of the events they all witnessed, but each one gives us a different view, because they journal from a personal perspective. Even though some of it may seem to be "just the facts", the writer is choosing to share the God-experiences that specifically impressed his heart. Much of the Bible can be viewed as God's inspired Word being passed through the journals of these faithful followers.

Although I want to address intentionally equipping children to participate in spiritual journaling, the principles are just as relevant for teenagers and adults. So, if you're not journaling, before you encourage your kids to start, try out some of the ideas and approaches yourself. There is great value in journaling... not only for today, but for tomorrow, and for years down the road.

Spiritual journaling ...

...helps to gain clarity. When you're having a difficult time understanding a concept or a scripture, writing down your random thoughts and then reviewing what you've written can be very insightful. It's like rotating a piece of a puzzle and when you hold it a certain way, you see where it fits all of a sudden. In times of confusion, journaling can be the instrument that God uses to help you sort out what questions you actually need to ask. What's not making sense? Where do I get lost? It's prayer in a form we're not accustomed to.

...provides a safe place. There's no ridicule or wrong in journaling. We have a big, mighty, powerful God who can handle our feelings; after all, He created them. The words penned there come from the heart. They may be very raw feelings, but they represent personal truth. It should be understood that journaling is private and it's something adults should respect. You wouldn't tell someone that their spoken prayer was wrong or needed correcting. Unless a child offers to share what's written there, the privacy of their journaling should be guarded.

When I journaled along with a group of kids, we regularly held each other accountable. Each time we met, I also gave them a chance to share something they had journaled. At first, very few of them read from what they had written, but after awhile, they really enjoyed sharing entries, especially those that were evidence of how they had worked through a particular issue. They recognized how God was working in their lives and were very comfortable sharing those journal entries. Although it's different from what we're used to, they were sharing their answers to prayer.

...is a storehouse for years to come. One of the most valuable aspects of journaling is being able to look back. A journal is a record of spiritual growth; it's a record of conversations with God. Through the comments and perspectives shared there, years later a child will be able to celebrate and embrace the journey God has taken him on. It's so rewarding to read about a spiritual struggle and then read months later how God has taken that incident and catapulted your spiritual understanding. That's why it's really important to date each entry in your journal. Without the words penned in the journal, it's easy to miss out on recognizing where the spiritual journey has actually taken you.

... helps you meditate on God's Word. Psalms 1:2 reminds us, *"... his delight is in the law of the Lord, and in His law he mediates day and night."* I think we all agree that it's a good thing to stop, get quiet, and just ponder what God's Word has to say ... not so easy for kids many times, though. Journaling can help kids, especially those who have a difficult time quieting their spirits, so they can meditate on Scripture. As they contemplate what to write, their minds are stretching and reaching for thoughts that are deeper than surface, off-the-cuff, "church-y" answers. In these moments, they pray through their written words, and are not on-the-spot to put their thoughts into words in the next ten seconds.

... fine tunes our spiritual sight. When you look for God at work in the world around you, you see Him. When a child knows that they will be journaling (talking with God), things that would normally go unnoticed are now God-sightings. Recognizing God moving in situations and lives that are near to the child is a source of spiritual strength and growth. Too often they don't tap into that source of strength simply because they don't notice. Journaling is a vehicle whereby kids pay attention and notice.

... articulates understanding and insights. Saying you understand something and being able to articulate it in the written word are two completely different things. Wrestling with words ... just the right word ... to say what it is that I'm actually thinking is mental exercise. But, as the words get rearranged and are hand-picked as a description, understanding of Scripture, expressing what is happening in your life, or something God is trying to teach a child comes into clearer view. Writing it down seems to help it make sense.

... is an expression of emotion. Journaling is a way for kids to vent their feelings to the Lord Himself. Understanding that what is written on the pages is between the child and God, and that God is big enough to handle any emotions that He created in us, can be a powerful tool for kids to have access to. Being able to express themselves, which may mean emotions that they're not proud of or feel like others would disqualify, very often gives them a handle on the emotions that seem so out of control. Many emotions function purely as a way of saying, "I want and need to be heard" and praying through journaling can satisfy that need.

In school, kids are usually given a prompt and ten minutes to write whatever they think about that pertains to that prompt. It could be a sentence starter and the child goes on to write a short story from there. Or, it might be an old adage, like "A bird in the hand is worth two in the bush" that the child has to free-write about. A spiritual journal is similar in that you're writing whatever you can mine from your brain and your heart, but the focus is different. It's important that the child keep in mind that there is a purpose to their spiritual journaling and that purpose is to keep them on their spiritual journey with God.

I'd like to suggest a variety of forms that spiritual journaling can take. Just like anything else you do all the time, if it's always the same, you tend to lose interest. If you jog every day, changing your route can make a big difference on how quickly the time passes and what you notice on the way. If you like to read, there's something special about the first day that's warm enough for you to sit on the patio, enjoying the sunshine, while you crack open a new book. In a similar way, you can change up journaling by doing a few simple things.

Provide different kinds of notebooks and writing utensils for the child to use. Kids who have a high word smart intelligence naturally love to play with words. But, one of the things that bring them additional joy when they write is being able to use a variety of papers and pens/markers/colored pencils. So, in August, when the stores are full of school supplies, purchase a few extra special writing elements that you can randomly present to the kids. You'll be pleasantly surprised at the boost this gives their journaling discipline.

Let the kids decorate and personalize the cover of their journal. The traditional college composition books (you know, the black and white books full of lined pages for your essay questions that always made you hyperventilate) make great journals for a couple of reasons. Right before school starts, you can usually purchase them for 25¢ ... that's a winner! And, the covers are sturdy enough that you can cover them with sticky paper or glue pictures on them without them disintegrating.

Encourage short-term types of journaling. Do a certain type of journaling for one month; then change. This gives the kids an opportunity to experiment with and find the type of journaling that is most beneficial to their personal spiritual growth. Some of these short-term journaling experiences are:

- **Book of the Bible.** The child will concentrate on reading one book of the Bible. Each day they will respond in their journal to what part of that particular book they read. It may be that during the month that they'll actually get through the book of the Bible more than once, which will reveal new insights in their second time through. What they write is a response to the love letter God has sent them.

- **God-sightings.** Every day the child will think about how they saw God working in the people or the situations around them. Wow! Wouldn't God love to hear how we see Him in action each day!

- **Prayer.** The kids will actually write—point blank—their prayers and how they see God answering prayer. Encourage them to write to God about their relationship with Him, rather than listing the things they want God to tend to. This is a "Dear God ..." journal.

- **I learned today.** This is one of my favorite things to journal. Every day I am aware that God is teaching me something. I'm also learning something new every day. Recognizing that I'm learning about God each day is an exciting thing to write about.

- **Random Scripture.** Take one verse. Read it and respond. Read it again and respond again. These verses don't have to be connected.

- **Spiritual theme.** Show the child how to use the concordance at the back of their Bible or one they can access online. Choose one topic and then read one of the verses listed under that topic each day. Respond to that verse.

- **Prompts.** When you present the child with a blank journal, already have a question written on each page. Make it something fairly general that will allow them to write in a variety of directions.

- **Seasonal.** Journal during the summer, Christmas, or Easter. There are special insights that can come through concentrating on what these special seasons mean in a child's life.

- **Online journaling.** Some sites, like YouVersion, have places on their Bible websites to keep a personal journal. What a fun way to change things up!

- **Sketch.** Younger children who cannot write fluently may want to sketch their journals. Or, once a week, a child can express themselves in their written journal by sketching what they are thinking about.

- **Verbal Journal.** Some children are so uncomfortable with writing that journaling is more of a negative experience than a positive one. There are some options for these kids. Voice-activated journaling is now possible through electronic devices. Using one of these instruments can give a child who struggles with writing the same experience through sharing verbally.

- **Video.** This is a wonderful option for kids who find writing difficult or who are just more verbal. Keeping a video journal can be done in private and has many of the same benefits ... if not more. Through video you can also see yourself, your body language, and you can talk faster than you could actually write down the thoughts.

Journaling can be great fun while helping kids grow closer to the Lord. Some kids will latch onto this spiritual discipline with excitement and others will shy away. Your responsibility is to introduce the possibilities and encourage your kids to find ways that help them connect to the One who created them. Journaling is definitely one of those great tools that they need to know about!

Tina is an editor, a writer, a speaker, a trainer, a coach, volunteer children's pastor, and loves all things kidmin, but her favorite title is Silly Grandma to 3 incredible grand-kiddos. You can check out what she's up to at tinahouser.net.

chapter 12

ALFRED G. SQUIRREL

Engaging Kids in Scripture Memorization

BY ELLEN HALEY

"Fix these words of mine in your hearts and minds; tie them as symbols on your hands and bind them on your foreheads. Teach them to your children, talking about them when you sit at home and when you walk along the road, when you lie down and when you get up. Write them on the doorframes of your houses and on your gates so that your days and the days of your children may be many" Deuteronomy 11:18-21a (NIV).

LET ME INTRODUCE YOU to Alfred G. Squirrel (the G standing for Grey). Alfred is your run-of-the-mill common gray squirrel, one like you might find in your back yard. He may be a common urban squirrel, but Alfred can teach you many things including how to engage children in "squirreling" away God's Word in their hearts and minds.

ACORN 1: SQUIRRELING AWAY GOD'S WORD IS IMPORTANT.

Alfred G. Squirrel was born with an instinct for storing food for the winter. From a young age, he understood the importance of preparing for times when food would not be readily available. How would he face the winter if this instinct for hiding away food failed to develop? How would he face the difficult times? It is this same degree of importance that you need to communicate to children.

Why is it important for children to engage in memorizing scripture? First, it is important because God demands it. In Deuteronomy 11:18a (NIV) God tells the people of Israel, *"Fix these words of mine in your hearts and minds."* He doesn't say, "If you feel like it, fix these words of mine on your heart." Instead, it is a command.

God's Word stored away in a child's heart is important also because it can be a source of comfort when they are facing difficult times. Through memorizing scripture, they will know how to share the good news of Jesus Christ. God's Word tucked away can help them resist when faced with a temptation to disobey God. Scripture can help them express praise and thanksgiving to the Lord in good times and bad. When you fail to help children store away nourishment for all times you're missing an important part of their spiritual development.

ACORN 2: IT SHOULD BE INTENTIONAL.

Alfred is an urban gray squirrel who is intentional in where he buries his nuts and other food—places he will be able to return to easily when winter arrives. This is important for Alfred. His life depends on it. It is with this intentionality that you should approach engaging children in scripture memorization. Their spiritual life depends on it.

Be intentional in planning for engaging children in committing scripture to memory and don't just use it as a filler activity when the lesson is too short or throw it into some activity because you know you should. It is more than just a few activities. Helping children build a lifelong habit of scripture memory will help them have a healthy and strong spiritual life. Deuteronomy 11:18-21 reiterates this need to be intentional. Teaching the next generation about God's Word is not something that happens by accident; it is an intentional part of life. The Israelites were to write God's Word on their doorframes and gates. They were to teach God's Word to their children at home and as they walked along the road. This didn't happen by accident and they did not have instant access to a Bible or to scrolls. The scripture was taught from memory and children learned to memorize it. It was intentional.

Have a master plan—a list of verses that are important for children to have hidden in their hearts as they grow. Keep in mind to have a variety of verses on your master list to provide balanced "nutrition." As you make your list, keep in mind Alfred G. Squirrel. He, like all squirrels, likes and needs variety in his diet. He may be found "squirreling" away all kinds of seeds and nuts, as well as different kinds of fruits. It is the same with children. They need variety in Bible verses that they commit to memory to provide balanced "nutrition." Choose verses that will be a help in a variety of situations—life struggles, joyful celebrations, and making tough choices. How do you form this list? The internet is a wonderful thing. There are numerous websites that have lists of essential verses for children to memorize. Utilize your curriculum. Keep a list of the memory verses from each lesson or unit. Your curriculum scope and sequence may also have some of these verses listed.

After you have a master list, come up with ways that you can incorporate these in your time with the children. Plan specific scripture memory emphasis and challenges throughout the church year. Each quarter or unit keep scripture memorization in mind as you plan lessons. Make sure it is a natural part of the lesson and not just an incidental part.

ACORN 3: KEEP AT IT.

An interesting thing about Alfred is that his teeth continue to grow throughout his life, and that's why squirrels are constantly gnawing and chewing. He has to keep at it. In order for kids to store away God's Word it needs to be taught and encouraged by both parents and the church. They have to keep at it.

How do we help parents engage their children in scripture memorization?

- Provide parents with tools they can easily use at home., such aslLists of memory verses that are important for children to know. Or make playlists on Spotify that have scripture memory songs so that parents can play them in the car or at home.

- Communicate with parents, letting them know IN ADVANCE the memory verses for the upcoming unit or lessons.

- Involve families in any planned memory verse challenges. Find ways that parents can set the example of memorizing scripture.

It is not just parents who can be involved in helping children fix God's Word in their hearts. Recruit volunteers to listen to the children recite their verses before, during, and after church. Get fun with it and give these special "listeners" fun t-shirts or badges. Make it a big deal for the kids to have to find people who are identified as "listeners" around the children's area or around the church. Several years ago, I recruited some of the youth in my church to be available before and after Bible study to listen to the children as they recite their verses. It was a growth experience for both the youth and the children (and the youth got cool t-shirts).

When recruiting volunteers, whether adults or youth, make sure you provide them with the verses ahead of time. Give them a chance to know the verses and set the example for the children.

ACORN 4: ENVIRONMENT IS KEY.

Unlike how it is portrayed in cartoons, squirrels do not hide all their food stores in a hollow tree. Instead, they make the most of the environment around them storing nuts in the ground, hidden behind objects, in discarded planters, or anywhere that is protected from other animals and is available. Squirrels may also go back to the same place multiple times to hide their food.

Utilizing your environment to the maximum is an important resource in helping children engage in scripture memorization. Think repetition, repetition, repetition. The more you see and hear something, the more likely you are to remember it. Imagine seeing and hearing a verse or a phrase everywhere you go, over and over. Are you going to remember it? (Think about the commercials you've seen or the song that repeats over and over the one phone number, 8675309.)

But how do you do it? Let your environment help you decide.

- Find song versions of the memory verses for a unit and play them as the students enter the children's area and in their classrooms.

- If you have lots of wall space, place posters with the memory verses in the classrooms as well as the hallways and entryways. Everywhere you can see a place for it, have the memory verse(s). At my church, we have a chalkboard in the hallway with the memory verse written on it in colorful chalk as well as written on boards and posters hung in the classrooms.

- Do you use a countdown PowerPoint? Why don't you make it a memory verse countdown, taking away or adding to the verse every second? When the verse is finished, it's time for the session to begin.

- Include the verse in the lesson whether a part of the Bible story or the application. Divide out the verse into phrases and write it on cards. Make sure each of the words/phrases is incorporated into the lesson. Pass out the cards and while the lesson is being shared, if the child with a card hears the words on his card, he/she takes the card to an assigned place. After the lesson, unscramble the cards as a class and discuss the verse.

- Get creative. Think of any way you can tie the verse into the children's environment. Use what you have.

Remember: repetition, repetition, repetition.

ACORN 5: KNOW THE LEARNER.

Just as there are many variations of squirrels spanning the globe, there are infinite types of children. Each child is a unique creation and learns in their own unique way. It is up to you to observe how your children learn the most effectively and then use their learning styles and interests to help them hide God's Word in their hearts.

Think about the ages of the children who you are ministering to. Choose verses that are understandable and appropriate for each level of learning without watering down God's Word.

Keep in mind that the youngest child can be learning scripture even if they are not yet able to "memorize" it. As a volunteer rocks an infant they can say scripture or sing a scripture song. When playing on the floor with toddlers, utilize scripture to reinforce what you're learning. Preschoolers love to find "lost" items around the room. Attach verses to cards, nature items, or toys. When the children bring you the "lost" item you read the verse to them.

Observation is key to deciding on activities to assist students in committing God's Word to memory. Observe your classes to see what types or activities they respond to positively. Games, math, puzzles, art, cooking, science, technology, drama, music, movement. There are numerous ways that kids love to learn. Offer varieties of activities where children can engage in memorizing scripture.

How do you do this?

- Learn a memory verse through cooking? Combine art and baking and decorate cookies or cakes with the memory verse, icing, and icing pens.

- Science object lessons provide ways for you to explain the meaning behind a verse.

- Kids who learn better by hearing? There are apps and online games where you can insert your memory verse and the kids can play the game. The Adventure Bible app allows you to read the scripture out loud. Students can look up the scripture and have it read to them. Another idea is to have each child read the memory verse into a recorder, but make sure they don't mention their name. Play the recording, making a game of it, and the children guess who is speaking each time. (Make sure that you write down each of the names in a list as they record it so you know the answer.)

- Invite someone to come in and teach the memory verse in sign language or find a video online of someone signing the verse.

- What about kids who love drama? Think about those commercials that are so catchy that you can repeat them almost word for word without realizing that you are learning it. So, the children can create a catchy commercial based on the memory verse. Let the kids be creative but with one stipulation, the complete verse must show up some place in the video.

- Do you need quiet activities as the children enter the room? Go to *puzzlemaker.discoveryeducation.com* and create puzzles around your memory verses or just google your verse and search for activity pages or coloring pages.

- Kids who love art? Provide a table filled with different art mediums, including clay, paint, canvases, and Legos with the only instructions being that they must depict the memory verse in art. Let go and let them create. You'll be surprised what the kids come up with. (And you can also get rid of some of those leftover art supplies that have overwhelmed your resource rooms.)

- Music? How about having the kids create their own movements to scripture memory songs or their own music video for the songs.

- Technology? You could download apps to a tablet so preschoolers can listen to the Bible verse being read. If you have access to multiple computers with Microsoft Office, divide a class of older children into small groups with one group per computer. The children will work together to create posters featuring the memory verse. For this you will need to set restrictions where they can go for pictures, but kids love being able to get creative with the computer. Another option is for the groups to create their own PowerPoint memory verse game and then have the whole class play the game.

- Nature? Do a nature walk and encourage children to pick up nature items that represent the memory verse. Give the children a large piece of construction paper or poster board with the words of the memory verse written on it in. Glue items from the nature walk around the letters.

- Do you have children who are competitive? Have a memory verse challenge over several weeks. The advantage of challenges is that they encourage a pattern of behavior (memorizing scripture) over an extended period. When a behavior is repeated enough it becomes habit. Through challenges we can encourage the formation of a habit of scripture memory.

Make sure the message of the scripture does not get lost in the creativity and fun. Every activity should be a driving force toward understanding and knowing the scripture and not simply memorizing a bunch of words.

CONCLUSION

Children engaging in scripture memory is an essential part of their spiritual development, much like a squirrel storing up food for the winter. It is a command of God and one that is not easy for everyone, but it is still a command. To everyone involved in children's ministry this needs to be a priority.

Having been handed her first teacher's book at age 13 and sent in with a class of 2-year-olds, **Ellen Haley** still continues in children's ministry well over 30 years later. A graduate of Southwestern Baptist Seminary in Fort Worth, Ellen has served in full, part-time, and volunteer ministry. She lives in Georgetown, TX and is the founder of FaithFit™ Ministry.

chapter 13

EVERYONE WINS
Engaging Kids in Serving

BY JOY CANUPP

E NGAGING CHILDREN IN SERVING opportunities is truly a win-win for everyone. Actually, it is a win for the whole world! So, if you want to be part of something much bigger than you can imagine, let's journey together to explore the reasons to give ample serving opportunities to children, the many who benefit, and a few of the zillion practical ways to create those experiences both inside and outside the church walls.

WHY BOTHER?

Folks who are around children even a little know that it's more time consuming to teach them how to do something versus just doing it themselves. To explain a task, give an example, be patient while the child makes attempts, explain again (and again) and model another time ... whew! ... it's exhausting just thinking it through. BUT. Do we really want to raise a generation of self-absorbed, self-centered, pew-sitting people who never extend a hand to serve their churches and communities? Of course not! So, let's make the extra effort on the front end while our children are young. Let's teach them that Jesus, as our ultimate example, came to serve (Mark 10:45). Let's make it fun. Let's make it part of their normal. And, let's not wait until they are "old enough."

IT'S NEVER TOO EARLY

There is not a minimum age requirement for serving. In carefully planning serving opportunities for kids and their families, we should include tasks that can be done by the very youngest in the bunch. As soon as they can walk and carry things in their little hands, they are ready to be "helpers" and serve others. Here are a few starter ideas.

- At church on the preschool hall - Use a soap and water mixture for little hands to wipe down tabletops, chairs, counters, and toys with fun brightly-colored sponges.

- Outside at church - Pick up sticks or pinecones and toss them in a bucket. This is not only a way for littles to serve, but also a way to get the wiggles out!

- At a park in the community - Give away stickers that say "Smile, God loves you!" This will engage the youngest in outreach ... and who can deny a sticker from a sweet chubby little hand?

- At home - Toss clothes in the washer, fold washcloths from the dryer, put away plastic containers from the dishwasher, and pick up toys. These are all age-appropriate ways that toddlers can help Mom and Dad.

For toddlers, these activities are fun and game-like. The key to including them in serving is the language the adults use when engaging them in these activities. Phrases such as: "You are being a good helper," "Thank you for helping at church/

home," and "You helped that nice man in the park get a smile today" are words that reinforce the serving concept to toddlers.

When serving opportunities are extended as early as the toddling years, it becomes very natural for kids to continue serving through elementary ages and beyond. So, ministry leaders, let's *"equip the saints for the work of ministry, for building up the body of Christ,"* Ephesians 4:12 (ESV) ... including the little ones!

EVERYONE TRULY WINS

Obviously, when someone is served in some way, there is a great benefit. From receiving a bottle of water from a child ... to having a car washed ... to being the recipient of an anonymous blessing basket of groceries left on the porch, the person on the receiving end definitely wins. And, in that, we are fulfilling the law of Christ (Galatians 6:2).

THE CHILD WINS

Short-term wins of serving include learning to give without receiving, learning to smile, learning to look others directly in the eye when speaking, and experiencing that "full heart" feeling when helping others in some way.

Long-term wins of serving include developing compassion for others, learning to see and meet needs practically, and growing up with minimal impact of worldly self-absorption.

Although a child will not yet know his gifts, he can learn to obey the Scripture that says *"as each has received a gift, use it to serve one another, as good stewards of God's varied grace"* 1 Peter 4:10 (ESV).

Consider this! Offer an "elite" serving opportunity for older kids. Using your ministry's oldest two grade levels is suggested so that the first year is a learning experience that can be refined during the second year. So, whether that is 4th/5th or 5th/6th in your setting, invite those children into a very special situation to elevate their practical serving opportunities. This may be incorporated into a Wednesday or Sunday evening time. It may be a during-the-week club option or it could even be worked into a Sunday morning. Whatever time you choose, make it regular and important. Invite the designated grades to submit an application to be part of the experience. Increase the value by also including brief interviews. Again, tailored to your own setting, you may actually end up with all of the kids in those grades as participants OR you may determine a certain number of spaces and limit the number of kids who can participate. Give this opportunity a special name. Give the kids special t-shirts. Be sure parents are on the same page with expectations that you have communicated. Once the structure is in place, the sky is the limit to serving opportunities that this group of older kids can be involved with both inside and outside the church walls. Who will hand out the bulletins? Well, it just may be this group of older kids!

Note that this concept will be tailored to meet each specific ministry area but is one that can be implemented no matter what your situation.

THE PARENT WINS

Parents are typically willing to accept all the help they can get on the challenging adventure of raising children. When the church creates serving opportunities for kids on a regular basis, parents will enjoy children who become less selfish, more cooperative, more considerate, and more giving. Sibling rivalry tends to decrease when children are given regular practice of putting others first. And opportunities for families to serve together strengthens the bond between parents and children through non-technology driven activity, which is an experience often difficult for today's parent to create themselves.

Consider this! Some churches have found that family serving opportunities make a great program on Sunday or Wednesday evenings. FamilyServe, Serving Together, or some other creative name gives children and at least one parent a time to regularly serve together. Good planning for this type of weekly or monthly experience is a must and is best done with a coordinator and team of folks. The basic concept is that families will show up at the designated time ready to serve in whatever capacity has been planned for them. Having the supplies, directions, and necessary arrangements made ahead of time is critical. Here are some ideas for this type of experience.

- Clean the church kitchen.
- Clean the preschool hall rooms/toys.
- Care for the church lawn by raking, picking up debris, and planting flowers.
- Refresh the pens and envelopes in the back of the worship center chairs.
- Create VBS decorations.
- Cut out/prep materials for upcoming Sunday morning children's classes.
- Place church info labels on water bottles ... so, the next serving time families can go to parks or malls to give them out.
- Take food items to the local food pantry and help shelve the donations.
- Deliver boxes of doughnuts to the police station, fire station, hospital, or other local community services.

THE CHURCH WINS

Ministry areas in all churches in all areas have a volunteer dilemma. Who will sign up for next Sunday? Who will man the coffee table? Who will hand out the bulletins? Who will take up the offering? Who will teach the littles? The amazing answer to many of these questions is that older children can fill so many of these needs. And, when that happens, the church wins! As adults make time to mentor and teach children the practical aspects of these serving opportunities, they receive much more than if they had just done it themselves. When you duplicate yourself in children, you are satisfying an immediate need as well as a long-term solution for the volunteer crisis as these kids enter adulthood. Serving will be their normal rather than a guilt-induced activity.

Consider this! Organize a mentor serving model in which kids are paired up with ushers, greeters, parking lot attendants, and others. For example, when someone is asked to be a Sunday morning greeter at the second service, he is trained and agrees to the basic responsibilities. He is also asked to agree to be a mentor for a child. On predetermined weeks, that greeter will be matched with a child who is learning to be a greeter. They will be at the assigned post together and share the greeting responsibilities. This could be duplicated in many areas around the church. The additional adult relationship in that child's life, the increased volunteer base, the dedication of the adult mentor, and the intergenerational experience are some incredible benefits of this model.

THE LOCAL COMMUNITY WINS

Beyond seeing "cute kids helping others," the community is often reminded that serving others is important. Adults, many whom may be unbelievers, are the recipients of God's love in action (Matthew 5:16) and are sometimes prompted to engage in serving and/or question their own motives and beliefs. The local area wins when children grow up thinking beyond themselves and look for ways to make a difference in their hometown.

Consider this! A Saturday morning of families serving together in various community projects such as washing police cars, cleaning up at parks or schools, and playing games with nursing home residents. After a couple of hours of projects, come back together for a quick lunch, time of celebration, and story-sharing before everyone heads home. If Saturday sports make this challenging for your area, consider the same format on a Sunday afternoon.

THE WORLD WINS

When future generations are being raised to respect others, to help others, to give freely, and to love unconditionally, the world wins. Imagine a world in which the new normal is to serve others with open hands and open hearts. Imagine when this infiltrates corporations and schools and governments. Imagine the possibilities that can occur several generations from now when you spend today engaging children in practical serving opportunities.

Consider this! When you're ready to take serving with children to a whole new level, plan a mission trip for families with older children. Create an experience in which participants will pack a bag, be away from home for 2-5 nights, and spend their days serving others in some capacity. It could be in another state or it could be several towns over. The children who have this opportunity will likely remember it for years and possibly point back to it as a marker in their spiritual journey.

HUMILITY AND JOY

With all of this winning happening when kids serve, your efforts may become a bit showy if you're not careful. As you instill servanthood in the next generation, teaching humility is important. You can talk about it plenty but one of the best teachers will be anonymity. When children do things without being known and without receiving credit for the deed, they will begin to understand the humble side of selfless serving.

And, kids should learn that serving with a smile is a must! Serving with a grumpy attitude is no good for anyone involved. Teaching through words and example that serving with joy is the preferred way is important. You may not always feel like serving. You don't always feel like smiling. You get to choose to do both and kids can learn that from a very early age.

Why humility and joy? *"Whatever you do, work heartily, as for the Lord and not for men, knowing that from the Lord you will receive the inheritance as your reward. You are serving the Lord Christ"* Colossians 3:23-24 (ESV).

EVEN MORE IDEAS

In addition to the many ideas sprinkled throughout the previous sections, here is a list to generate even more creativity to tailor to your setting and families you minister with.

- Make and mail cards to missionaries, folks in elected government positions, and active military personnel.
- Make cards and goody bags for nursing homes. Take them and visit with the residents.
- Assemble care packages for the homeless.
- Pack shoeboxes for Operation Christmas Child.
- Bake cookies for school teachers, church staff, police/ fire stations.
- Take a walk through your Main Street area and ask store owners "How can we pray for you today?"
- Vacuum and sweep the church halls.
- Sort preschool supplies and help by throwing away broken crayons and testing the markers.
- Create a fun bag for children in the hospital.
- Wash cars for free at a park while people are playing. Wash the church vans/bus.
- Clean church windows.
- Sanitize door knobs at church (especially good during flu season).
- Visit shut-ins. Sing for them. Play games with them.
- Create placemats for local free meal agencies.
- Assist with preparations for the next big church event.

FINALLY, CONSIDER THIS!

Consider spending a block of uninterrupted time to do some creative thinking and planning in this area. Take this chapter and other resources that you gather to really pour over. Dive deep as you ponder your church dynamics, your community, and your families. Do you have parents who are passionate about teaching their kids to serve? Make a list and ask them to join you on this planning journey. As in other areas of ministry, build a team and watch those joint efforts do far more than you could do alone. Don't hesitate to start small and grow this area as you have successes and generate excitement with your families.

Take some time. Pray. Plan. Determine to develop a strategy for engaging kids in serving both inside and outside the church walls. Your kids, your church, your community, your world ... everyone ... will win!

Joy Canupp served as Children's Minister for 15 years in a SC church and is now encouraging/supporting folks in ministry through retreats, speaking, and blogging at *Leading With Joy* (joycanupp.com). She loves spending time with family and friends, thrifting, playing games, and all things purple!

chapter 14

TRACKS, YOGURT, AND ACCOUNTABILITY

Engaging Kids in Daily Devotions

BY STEPHANIE CHASE

I N SIXTH GRADE the student pastor in our small church announced the big news, "We're going to the beach!" I was excited. I mean ecstatic! Going to the beach with my youth group? What more could a sixth grader want?

Being from an East Texas town, the beach was anything better than a catfish infested lake. You're probably imagining a motley country youth group venturing to the beautiful blue waters of Gulf Shores, Alabama or the gorgeous white sandy beaches in Florida. No, not us. We loaded into the ragged old beat-up church van and headed straight to the brown beaches and dirty water of Galveston. (I can say that because I live in Houston!) It was heaven! All we imagined and more.

I soon discovered the tricks of a wise minister. My student pastor used these beautiful beaches as a lure. We didn't spend countless hours laying on the beach, tanning, playing volleyball and frisbee. Instead, he arranged for a trendy young speaker to meet with us morning, noon, and night. The guest had one goal ... teach kids how to spend time with Jesus daily and love it! The faithful minister plowed through session after session teaching this energetic and rather homely group of preteens how to have a quiet time.

When I boarded the van headed to Galveston, I had no idea the weekend would forever change my life. I chose to follow Jesus at the age of eight. I attended church regularly and participated in all of the programs. I sang the songs and recited the verses. What I discovered on the shores of Galveston was a very profound truth ... a major piece of my relationship with Jesus was missing—daily devotion.

The speaker during that weekend was smart. After teaching us how to engage in this daily discipline, he offered the material we needed to continue when we got home. He gave us papers with scriptures to read and journals to jot down our thoughts. Prayer pages were handed out to document how God answered. Small cards with verses to memorize were placed in our hands. It was the complete package and that package was what I needed to begin a daily quiet time with God.

After a sweaty non-airconditioned van ride home, with sunburned shoulders and a heart eager and full, I entered my bedroom, placed all of my new materials and Bible beside my bed. I committed on that trip to spend time with Jesus and that's what I was determined to do. Each morning I got up and prayed, read God's Word, and journaled where I saw God at work through prayer. What made me passionate about my daily time with Jesus? Let's learn.

GIVE KIDS TRACKS TO RUN ON.

The Bible is a big confusing book for kids. Most adults don't understand how it all fits together. How can children? We all need a Bible reading plan. When children know what to read, they are equipped to start.

PROVIDE THE PLAN.

Think proactively about the tracks you are laying. When a road is built, engineers determine in advance the destination of the highway. Roads are constructed with intention and purpose. The Bible reading plan given to children in your ministry needs a destination with purposeful, calculated intent. Daily devotions can meet the spiritual goals set for your children. Provide intentional scriptures for your kids and families to read daily.

Questions to consider as you lay tracks.

- Can the Bible reading plan align with kids' worship teaching?
- Should the Bible reading coincide with small group lessons?
- In what areas do your children need more Bible teaching—Old Testament, New Testament, the life of Jesus?
- Is there a topical study appropriate for circumstances in this season of your community?
- Do you have time to create the reading plan?
- Is it better to use pre-written plans?
- Should you include families in the Bible reading or target children only?

No matter what tracks you choose to lay, be intentional. Next, consider yogurt and accountability.

CONSIDER YOGURT AND ACCOUNTABILITY.

The first few months after the transforming weekend on Galveston Island, I was faithful to spend time with Jesus daily. I was up before school, praying for classmates, learning more from God's

Word. As time passed, however, the newness started to wear off. I became a little lazy and before you know it, the passion to read and pray was gone. My daily devotion to Jesus waned. My journal was empty and God's Word ceased to saturate my soul daily.

Mrs. Skinner, who went as a sponsor to Galveston, noticed the investment of budget money and purposeful intention of the weekend trip vanishing quickly. The precious middle-aged lady made one wise move that still impacts my life to this day.

One Wednesday evening after the preteen group met, Mrs. Skinner gathered a cluster of gangly preteen girls and asked a simple transforming question. "Girls, how are you doing on your quiet times?" Of course, none of us made eye contact. We looked to the ground and hung our heads in shame.

"I think I know why we're all struggling," Mrs. Skinner replied.

"Why?" we chimed together regaining confidence knowing we had drifted from the commitment made just a few months earlier.

"Accountability," she said with excitement.

We looked at each other in confusion. This was a new word for us.

"Accountability? What did that mean?" we wondered.

"Let's start meeting at church every Monday night during church visitation," Mrs. Skinner suggested. "We'll visit guests from the church, get yogurt, and talk about our time devoted to the Lord."

Mrs. Skinner knew the key to discipline—accountability. Have you ever tried to lose weight and not told anyone? Have you ever tried to lose weight when you must weigh in each week? What's the difference? John Maxwell says, "The things we are held accountable for, we do well." Why is accountability important in engaging children in daily devotion? Because you want them to do it well and for a lifetime.

Why do you want children to spend time daily with Jesus reading God's Word? Look at the benefits and blessings when they do.

"Do not conform to the pattern of this world, but be transformed by the renewing of your mind. Then you will be able to test and approve what God's will is—his good, pleasing and perfect will" Romans 12:1-2 (NIV).

"I have hidden your word in my heart that I might not sin against you" Psalm 119:11 (NIV).

" ... whose delight is in the law of the Lord, and who meditates on his law day and night. That person is like a tree planted by streams of water, which yields its fruit in season and whose leaf does not wither—whatever they do prospers" Psalm 1:2-3 (NIV).

"Keep this Book of the Law always on your lips; meditate on it day and night, so that you may be careful to do everything written in it. Then you will be prosperous and successful" Joshua 1:8 (NIV).

Mrs. Skinner was a genius when she asked this powerful question. She said two words that hooked us for sure, "get yogurt." What preteen doesn't want to get yogurt or Starbucks or ice cream?

The next week the monumental life-changing series of meetings began. Five ordinary East Texas girls were dropped off at the church by their parents. Fighting over "shotgun" (that's the front seat), we loaded up in Mrs. Skinner's car and traveled our small city visiting guests. After many strikeouts visiting, our favorite part of the night approached. We buckled in and headed to the yogurt place in town. After much giggling and senseless preteen girl chat, Mrs. Skinner drove us back to church. Each Monday night, we sat on the floor in an adult Sunday school class and learned the priceless impact accountability can have on a life, and most importantly, on a relationship with Jesus.

Mrs. Skinner began each Monday accountability night by asking a simple, non-threatening question, "What did you read in the Bible this week?" As each girl shared her thoughts on the verses read throughout the week, deep questions surfaced. We wrestled with fears and uncertainties about our faith. It was a safe place to say, "I don't understand what the Bible means." With each Monday meeting our faith grew stronger and our love for Jesus increased.

Now don't let me fool you. There were many nights in the midst of a serious theological discussion one girl would get the giggles and the rest was history. Other nights the talk shifted to boys or the trending music or movies. No matter where the conversation went, Mrs. Skinner let us enjoy the conversation knowing we had found a safe place to be transparent. Somehow, our gentle and patient teacher always found a way to show us what God said about each subject.

After our discussion around the Word, it was time to pray. Each girl shared prayer requests. We prayed out loud for one another. We prayed for dogs that died, sick grandparents, good grades, and help on tests. The longer we met, though, the more serious our prayers became. The time we spent together increased our trust in one another and the result was transparency in prayer.

During that season of accountability and prayer time, I saw God work for the first time in my life. Mrs. Skinner shared with us that her husband was not a follower of Jesus. As a sixth-grade girl, I never prayed for a person to give their life to Jesus. I grew up in the church, but some way I missed praying specifically for lost people.

There we were, strange, awkward, silly preteen girls praying every Monday night for Mr. Skinner to ask Jesus into his heart, to accept Jesus Christ as Savior and Lord. This was a huge prayer for the girl who before Galveston had only thanked God for food at dinner and for a good day at bedtime.

I wasn't kidding when I said yogurt and accountability transformed my relationship with Jesus. God answered our prayer. I'll never forget when Mr. Skinner gave his life to Jesus. His salvation was my first experience seeing God at work in a really big way. I watched Mr. Skinner grow in his relationship with God, serve in our church, and eventually join us on random weekend trips that our pastor lured us into by some crazy gimmick. Those weekend trips, though, created a spiritual discipline that has grown five gawky girls into beautiful women who love the Lord with all their hearts. Each one of the girls, the Monday night motley crew, still to this day, 30 years later, love God and are committed to Him.

Do you really want to know how to make daily devotions engaging for kids? Tracks, yogurt, and accountability.

- Kids want to talk.
- Kids want to be heard.
- Kids will read God's Word when they are given tracks to run on and held accountable.
- Find ways to hold kids accountable.
- Form groups that include: a leader, a small group of kids, clearly defined Bible reading plan, something fun, and time to talk and pray.

ENGAGE LEADERS WHO LOVE KIDS AND GET THE VISION

Invite adults or college-age people to lead a kids accountability group. Share the vision. Last summer a college sophomore, hosted an accountability group at the gym for boys in the kids' ministry at our church. What boy doesn't want to play basketball with a cool college student? After running up and down the court the boys got into the Word and prayed together. It was male yogurt and accountability.

Leaders must be flexible. Kids will be kids. Children get off topic, giggle, and pick their noses. Don't give up. Love them, listen, and lead them to daily take up their cross and follow Jesus. Care deeply and show that each child is special to you. When kids know you care in spite of their kid factor that sometimes gets out of control, they will come. The more they come, the more they learn. The more they learn, the more they grow. The more they grow, the closer they are to Jesus. That is your ultimate goal.

TAKE IT BEYOND THE CHURCH WALLS.

Do activities with the group at times other than the weekly meeting. An accountability group of elementary kids meets every Thursday after school at a centrally located Starbucks near the church for an hour. Parents help the kids get a snack and then moms and dads hit the road. The kids talk about the daily Bible reading given out each Sunday in kids' ministry. The leader takes the given tracks and excites the group about their daily devotion to Jesus. If you stop by the Starbucks, you'll see kids praying, reading, laughing, and oftentimes doing a lot of "off topic" talking.

Close to the beginning of summer, this Starbucks accountability group spent the night at the leader's farm 3+ hours away from our city. The children played outside, swam in the pond, fished, and roasted marshmallows. Each time I see one of those accountability kids, they immediately talk about the memories made on the trip.

Do you want to engage kids in daily devotions? Let me encourage you to ...

LAY THE TRACKS.

1. Determine a Bible reading plan for the children in your ministry.

2. Deliver the Bible reading plan in a variety of ways: Facebook, email, give out at church. Ensure every child has access to the plan.

3. Keep it simple. Use pre-written daily devotion literature. When writing your own, suggest 3-5 verses for children to read daily and no more.

BEGIN GROUPS

1. Form an accountability group with children yourself. Attempt the process first.

2. Cast the vision to your ministry team. Imagine each child engaged in daily devotions.

3. Empower leaders to use yogurt/basketball/their own creative lure and accountability.

INCLUDE ESSENTIALS

Ensure the following three requirements in each accountability group:

1. Bible Reading - Expect each child to read the Bible. Discuss what each child learned.

2. Prayer - Share prayer requests. Expect each child to pray out loud.

3. The Fun Factor - Plan a special place to meet or a fun snack.

Statistics are startling about the positive effects of daily devotions on children's long-term spiritual growth and commitment. Time with Jesus in the Word and prayer is a must for every child. Determine today to make engaging children in daily devotions a priority. Who knows? One day, a hyper little second grader or a shy timid fourth grader may write a chapter on the greatest kids' minister ever ... the one who lured them in to discover a major piece of their relationship with Jesus—daily devotions.

Stephanie Chase is a graduate from Texas Tech University and received her master's degree from Southwestern Baptist Theological Seminary. She has worked in education and kids' ministry as a teacher, director, writer, and trainer for over 20 years and currently serves as the Kids' Minister at Champion Forest Baptist Church. She is passionate about inspiring you to live the life God has planned for you through leading family conferences, women's events, and leadership trainings.

chapter 15

EVEN AN EAR BONE MAKES A DIFFERENCE

Engaging Kids in Their Spiritual Gifts

BY LINDA WEDDLE

"We have different gifts, according to the grace given to each of us. If your gift is prophesying, then prophesy in accordance with your faith; if it is serving, then serve; if it is teaching, then teach; if it is to encourage, then give encouragement; if it is giving, then give generously; if it is to lead, do it diligently; if it is to show mercy, do it cheerfully" Romans 12:6-8 (ESV).

W E HAD EIGHT summer Sunday nights to do something unique with a group of 20-30 first through sixth graders. Most of these kids had grown up in the church and our goal was to present them with curriculum that was both challenging and unique.

Our choice? Eight weeks of the kids being introduced to different staff members and volunteers who were part of our church ministry. Some of the people we invited to speak were: a board member, the visitation pastor, the treasurer, and the lady who regularly laundered the dirty crib sheets from the nursery.

Although not all our guests considered themselves adept at relating to kids, they took the responsibility seriously and did a great job. The church treasurer even offered to give the kids their own set of offering envelopes (with their parents' permission) and several kids took him up on it. (Yes, many people give online, but we thought it would be a more tangible activity if the kids used envelopes. That way they could collect their own money and bring it to church themselves.)

We saw the kids get excited about being involved in their church. One boy told me that he prayed that someday he could serve on a church board. After listening to someone from the maintenance crew, kids were also more conscientious about throwing away candy and gum wrappers rather than dropping them on the floor. When the visitation pastor spoke, the kids asked if they could paint pictures for him to give to the housebound members he visited each week.

Throughout the summer, the kids were able to see how people used their different spiritual gifts to minister together. At the end of the program, a few kids asked if we could do it again and hear even more staff members talk. What had started as a plan for a summer activity has resulted in the kids having a new perspective on their church.

Whether you oversee a large ministry staff or whether you are a teacher of an individual class, introducing kids to the spiritual gifts should be on your list of priorities. These kids whose lives you touch are not the church of tomorrow, but the church of today.

DEFINITIONS

And, our first step is defining the term.

Think about it. To most kids, a gift is something they receive at Christmas or at their birthday and is most often a toy or game that's been on their wish list. They don't think of a gift as something intangible, so the concept must be defined in a simple, understandable, kid-friendly way.

One definition: A spiritual gift is an ability given to us by God, so that we can reflect His love in sharing the Gospel of Jesus Christ to those around us.

Once a definition is established, ask the kids what they think their spiritual gift is. (At this point, since you have not listed the actual gifts, you might find it interesting to hear what they say.) Discuss: What spiritual gifts do you think the people in our church have? Think about the pastor, your teacher, your parents? What spiritual gifts do you think you have? What spiritual gifts would you like to have?

Once you've defined a spiritual gift, you need to define the individual gifts. For the purpose of this chapter, I will use the list in Romans 12.

1. Prophesying – telling forth the truth. Prophesying is not so much telling the future as it is speaking the truths of God's Word. Most pastors do this through their sermons or when they're helping someone on a one-to-one basis. They study Scripture so they can explain God's Word, they warn against sin, and they encourage godly living.

2. Serving – including service of many types, but here serving seems to have an emphasis on helping the poor or needy.

3. Teaching – studying God's Word and explaining its meanings; teaching others how to apply scriptural truths to their lives.

4. Encouraging – building others up by giving them courage. This could mean encouraging them toward their goals or helping them through a tough time.

5. Contributing – giving not only of one's own possessions/money but also wisely distributing the money of the church.

6. Leading – guiding others to make right choices, to accomplish goals, inspiring them to do their best, and to use their own spiritual gifts.

7. Showing mercy – displaying kindness to others, especially those in need. Recognizing someone's need and helping out.

Discuss: Now that we've talked about the spiritual gifts, are the ones you mentioned listed? From this list, which one(s) do you think you have?

WHY ARE THE SPIRITUAL GIFTS IMPORTANT?

Though some kids might have heard about the spiritual gifts, others will have no idea what they are. Here are some ways the importance of the gifts can be explained.

1. Read through the following verses and ask the kids what they think they mean. (The verses should be somewhat easy to explain, especially for older kids.) Emphasize that we are the "parts."

"Just as a body, though one, has many parts, but all its many parts form one body, so it is with Christ. Even so the body is not made up of one part but of many. Now if the foot should say, 'Because I am not a hand, I do not belong to the body,' it would not for that reason stop being part of the body. And if the ear should say, 'Because I am not an eye, I do not belong to the body,' it would not for that reason stop being part of the body. If the whole body were an eye, where would the sense of hearing be? If the whole body were an ear, where would the sense of smell be? But in fact God has placed the parts in the body, every one of them, just as he wanted them to be." 1 Corinthians 12:12, 14-18 (ESV).

2. Has a child been vocal about a recent injury? (Many kids enjoy talking about their bruises.) If the child is fairly outgoing, interview her.

When did you get your bee sting? Did it hurt? Right after it stung you, did you go play with your friends or did you complain to your mom or dad about how much it hurt? How did you get it to stop hurting?

One small sting, not even this big (hold up your fingers), can make your whole body miserable. That's just like the body of Christ. As Christians, we are all part of that body and when one part is hurting or doesn't show up or do his job, the entire body hurts.

3. Show a diagram of the three smallest bones in the body (diagrams are easy to find on the internet)—those that make up the inner ear. The stapes is the tiniest of these and is less than half the size of your pencil eraser. Yet, if these bones don't function, the entire body is affected; people can't hear or they get off balance and are too dizzy to do anything! The dysfunction of that small bone has an impact on the function of the entire body.

4. Show (or show video clips) of other examples of things not working because of one missing part: a car with a dead battery, a chair with three legs, a chocolate chip cookie recipe without the chocolate chips.

Explain how it is the same within a church. If the pastor is not preaching from the Bible, if the teacher doesn't show up, if the maintenance crew lets the grass grow as high as the second floor, the entire church hurts. Likewise, if a church member is unkind, argumentative, or hateful, the entire body of Christ hurts.

As each person (part) uses their individual gifts, the church body remains healthy and vibrant.

WHICH GIFT IS MINE?

Now that kids have some idea of the spiritual gifts and what they are, some may be asking you how they know which one is theirs. A lot of spiritual gift surveys are available, some of them for kids. But here's an opportunity to involve the parents and do your own informal surveys. (Parents might discover their spiritual gifts, too!)

Ask the children questions such as the following:

- What do you enjoy doing the most?
- What do you want to do as an adult?
- If we were planning a big party, what job would you want to have? (Making the food, greeting the guests, leading the activities)
- Do you like to make new friends? What do you say to someone the first time you meet him or her?
- What was your favorite activity we did in class this past year?

Even with the most conclusive survey possible, you often can't identify a child's gifts. Kids change as they mature or as they have different experiences. On the other hand, some kids very clearly show evidence of their gifts from a young age.

What you can do as a leader/teacher of children, is encourage them to follow the leading of the Holy Spirit and also give them opportunity to use their gifts.

1. Be positive. Sometimes kids tell you what they want to do with their lives and you may discourage them by your response. One sentence can change a child's attitude. You can destroy a child's aspirations by telling him you don't think he's capable of doing something that he truly wants to do. On the other hand, one sentence of encouragement can make a lifelong impact.

2. Give them opportunity. Plan events or create situations where kids can serve in different capacities. Put one child in charge of leading the games, another in charge of explaining the schedule, still another in charge of welcoming visitors. If you have a child who enjoys technology, ask him to design a computer program for your class.

As you watch the kids fulfill their tasks, you should notice who does well at their responsibility and think of ways you can encourage the child to mature in that role.

You should also do outside-of-church service events. You can take the kids to a nursing home to greet the residents. You can collect food for a food bank, rake leaves, or weed flower beds in the homes of church members who can no longer do those things themselves.

3. Skype or Facetime with missionaries or people who are serving in different capacities so they see the wide variety of roles in which someone can serve.

4. Be aware. If you notice a kid being friendly to a visitor, thank him for his kindness. If you see a kid volunteering to help a teacher move chairs or set up game equipment, thank him for his help. If you see a child helping when another child trips and falls, let her know you noticed her concern. In addition, mention the situation to the parents. "Heather, Noah went out of his way to welcome the visitor we had tonight. He did a great job making the new boy feel at home." When you encourage the parent, you're accomplishing two things, because parents always tell their children what was said.

5. Set up a shadow program. Arrange for kids to shadow those in the church who are in ministry. When you have a fifth grader who wants to be a pastor someday, you can arrange for him to hang out with the pastor for an afternoon. When you have a fourth grader who has a passion for helping the needy, you can let her tag along with the Hunger Team to deliver food to the needy. When you have a child who wants to teach, you can ask a teacher to include him in her lesson preparation and delivery.

6. Visit Christian organizations nearby. Many Christian organizations give tours or welcome visits from church groups. Plan field trips where kids are able to see first hand what goes on. If possible, arrange for kids to ask questions of an employee.

7. Give kids regular responsibilities in church.

- picking up trash/worship folders after a service
- ushering/door greeter
- setting up or taking down chairs
- passing out supplies
- helping organize food or clothes that were donated for a shelter
- working with the sound technician
- writing a play or dramatization
- assisting a teacher in giving a lesson
- writing a note of kindness to someone who is ill
- accompanying adults in visiting a child who hasn't attended for a while
- leading a small group in reading a portion of Scripture or in answering questions
- be a big sister/brother to a younger child

With the parent, come up with a time commitment. A month is a good place to start. (After a month, kids can change jobs or move up a level to more responsibility in their current role.) Kids, parents, and church reps sign a contract stating the child's responsibility and that he/she will complete the task. Somewhere on the contract have a statement that reads something like: _____ is an usher, an important part of the ministry of First Community Church.

You should give kids opportunities to serve in different capacities, to encourage them when they're a good fit, and to patiently understand that some kids won't find their niche until much later in life. (That doesn't mean they can't serve now.)

As a children's ministry leader and teacher, you need to be alert to each child's abilities, give them every opportunity to perfect those abilities, and be an encouragement as they move forward.

Because **Linda Weddle** spent many childhood hours listening to her author father dictate kids' adventure stories to her mom, she decided she wanted to be a writer *before* she could even read, and that's what she's been doing ever since. She drinks a lot of iced tea, takes a lot of pictures, and once was rudely interrupted by a herd of wild horses while she was telling a story to 160 campers on the bank of Montana's Boulder River.

chapter 16

MOVE MOUNTAINS

Engaging Kids in Leadership

BY LISA DAVIS

"You're off to Great Places!
Today is your day!
Your mountain is waiting,
So ... get on your way!"

THIS QUOTE FROM Dr. Seuss' book, *Oh, the Places You'll Go,* helps remind me of the huge potential of kids. His books, although zany, always seem to inspire kids to step out to influence the world. How do you help kids climb their mountains? Simply begin to let them lead! Find someone who believes in a child, who can see their potential, and then give them opportunities to grow. The adults in my life did just that. My dad let us occasionally lead worship on stage as a family early on. I also taught alongside my mom in children's church and VBS. She coached me and my siblings to give the puppet show, enact dramas, and help teach the craft. This allowed me to understand that God's grace will take kids to places they hadn't planned to go and to do what they could never do alone!

As leaders of children, those in your care are waiting, wondering just how God will use them. Jesus is calling them. He will help them rise into leadership and gain the skills needed to serve Him. God can and will use young people right now. God reminds you of this in Jeremiah.

> *"Before I formed you in the womb I knew you, before you were born I set you apart; I appointed you ... I said, 'I do not know how to speak; I am too young.' But the Lord said to me, 'Do not say, 'I am too young.' You must go to everyone I send you to and say whatever I command you. Do not be afraid of them, for I am with you and will rescue you,' declares the Lord"* Jeremiah 1:4-8 (NIV).

Oh, the places kids will go! They can go to places that are off limits to adults and into unique communities to bring influence, such as on a playground, in a school room, at a ballet class, in their neighborhood, or on the soccer field. They can be a powerful force that God can use to further His kingdom. Let's equip them for success! Dr. Seuss' amazing story titles can inspire you as you go!

HORTON HATCHES THE EGG

Engaging Kids to Innovate and Hatch Great Ideas

Kids are pretty amazing. We often underestimate their potential and place them in a category of, "What do you want to do when you grow up?" I think the question needs to change to: "What do you want to do right now?" The only way you're going to allow them to influence this generation right now is if you believe in them. If you empower them to rise up.

One way to do this is by building a leadership team of students who want to serve and grow closer to God. Use an application to select or invite certain kids who seem to have an interest in leading. However, you certainly could make it open for all kids or kids in a certain grade. Create a plan to teach them about service and equip and excite them to see the vision that they can make a difference. Go through a leadership Bible study together, such as *Dare to Be a Daniel,* and teach them how to serve, share, and tell others about Jesus. Then put them into real roles of leadership.

Take it even further and have a brainstorming session as to what problems need to be solved in your church or community. Let the kids attack this problem collectively in their own way and have them generate ideas and solutions to solve the problem. You'll be surprised at their thinking and how they will bring energy and passion to this task. This kind of a program can possibly take place in the summer, during school breaks, or in a short elective series. Let them move some mountains!

HORTON HEARS A WHO!

Engaging Kids in Leadership through Compassionate Giving

Recently our church began a new giving campaign. Since we're a growing city, we decided as a body of believers to impact our community in an even greater way. We thought the kids in our elementary program could be some of the first givers and lead the way for the adults. When presenting this to the kids we talked about how Jesus told adults to become like kids if they want to know Him—that kids can lead the way and inspire others. We emphasized: "... *God loves a cheerful giver"* 2 Corinthians 9:7 (NIV). Banks were created and sent home. Everyone prayed. One child, after talking through everything with her parents decided to generously give 50% of her allowance totaling more than $300 over the next 3 years. Another student decided to give $100 of his savings. Together the kids and some of their leaders were able to generously donate over $3,000 and were excited to present this to the congregation to set an example of faithful giving. Kids not only can lead, but they can lead well.

MR. BROWN CAN MOO, CAN YOU?

Music: Songs of Hope and Prayer

Early in life children begin to imitate adults in song and prayer. Music repeatedly pulls you though the darkness and brings you healing. Many children are gifted musically and can use this gift to lead others. Put them to work! Kids can work alongside their parents or grandparents to lead young classes in worship. Kids can step up to lead their peers. Kids can play rhythm instruments to add another layer to the songs (beating a drum box or adding a tambourine are easy and fun)! Kids can sing in the adult service. Let them. Encourage this. Suggest it. It builds confidence and lifelong hope. Praise songs will be songs of hope to the cheerful and hurting for a lifetime.

Another way to see kids develop as worship leaders is by allowing them to use their musical gifts and talent to perform skits or dramas. Keep it as simple as possible and include a variety of roles. Using costumes, props, and puppets adds interest! This can be a great way to help kids learn to depend on God before, during, and after the service. Use technology to enhance the experience by adding pictures, music, and special effects. It's a wonderful way to include everyone.

PRAYER

Jesus opened a powerful window to you when He conquered death and sin. The curtain was torn and you could now approach God. The Bible also tells you *"... The prayer of a righteous person is powerful and effective"* James 5:16b (NIV). But you often struggle with prayer, typically neglecting this very powerful discipline when things are smoothly sailing along in life or if you're a little disappointed or upset with God. Engage kids to become prayer leaders! Form a kids' prayer team. Let them take prayer requests, give them prayer journals, encourage them to pray during the week. Perhaps, put up a prayer wall and have your team pick prayers to pray over during the week. Teach this special prayer leadership group ways to pray: praying scripture, prayers for missionaries, prayers for the city, prayer journaling, praying while creating art, sentence prayers, and circle prayers. Entrust kids to pray for the church and open your eyes to see mountains He will move!

THE CAT IN THE HAT

Engaging Kids in Leading at Celebrations and Events!

One of the best ways to allow kids to experience leadership is by letting them try on many different hats! One-time celebrations and events are perfect opportunities. By trying out different roles, they can refine their gifts! *"For we are God's handiwork, created in Christ Jesus to do good works, which God prepared in advance for us to do"* Ephesians 2:10 (NIV). After leading at events, students come away feeling confident and excited about themselves and understand more completely what it means to be willing servants. Students can even join in with planning, invitations, thank-you notes—experiencing the whole process.

Here are some ways they can serve:

- set up or clean up
- serving food
- help run an activity station
- decorating or displaying their artwork
- welcoming guests
- sorting and passing out supplies
- bounce house assistance
- Events kids could serve at:
    - Brunch or tea (with angels, grandparents, holidays)

- Community Outreach (Harvest Party, Christmas, Egg Hunts)
- VBS or summer camps
- Special Events (Paint and Praise Night, Donuts and Dads, Moms and Muffins, Missions Fair)
- Leadership Talent Show

After kids have had some serving success move them into more consistent service.

IF I RAN THE ZOO

Leadership on Sunday

Give the kids in your program regular opportunities to serve on Sunday. Keep it simple. Let them know they can serve Jesus every week. When kids have a leadership assignment on Sunday, they won't want to miss. They will show up and be ready to do the job.

Regular Sunday jobs could include, but are not limited to:

- first time guest buddies
- special needs friend
- craft assistant
- tech support
- read to younger students
- prayer, music, drama leaders
- small group leaders in a younger age group
- give directions
- give announcements
- birthday celebration assistant
- parking lot greeter
- help to give guests a tour

- collect offering
- guest storyteller
- teach a skill
- pray up front
- help in the adult service

Remember to find a place for the quiet leaders, too. Some kids don't enjoy interacting with people, but love to work behind the scenes. These activities work great for kids with special needs as well. Creating a spot for all different kinds of kids is important. Maybe someone is quiet, but gifted at art or writing. Look for opportunities to let them shine!

Quiet jobs:

- count offering money
- pass out papers
- gather supplies
- prep supplies
- turn the lights on and off
- draw pictures for a story
- sharpen pencils
- take photographs (stop animation, or Power-Point presentations)
- design a game to play
- work on a class scrapbook
- bring props on stage and off
- straighten up chairs
- sweep the floors
- sticky tag collector
- cleaning up after snack
- class t-shirt or logo designer

When using student leaders, training is of utmost importance. Set them up for success. Help them know what they will be doing, what their role is, practice if needed, and inspire them to be a quality leader. Before a big event, appoint a student leader trainer, who not only trains the kids but also supervises and gives feedback to them during and after the event. This should be someone who is relatable and loves working with kids. Taking the training and supervision off of your plate helps you as a leader to focus on other aspects during the event. Here are things to make sure you include in training young leaders: make the training fun, give encouragement, let them know what to expect and ways to help, provide feedback, collaborate together, and help them feel part of the team. Remember to celebrate with them after all the hard work is done.

GO, DOG, GO!

Building Kid Leaders Through Family Service

In this entitled world where some might feel they have been cheated out of something, and regularly feel "less than", true, faithful, serving is the remedy for their brokenness. When you give purely, you find yourself so close to Jesus.

Engaging whole families in short-term mission service activities is something that your church should consider. Something special happens when families give up their time to work side-by-side with one another to minister to a group in need. Kids are empowered and inspired in their leadership ability when they see that they had a role in completing something really big. Some possibilities are:

1. Bring a mobile VBS to a community that wouldn't normally get one

2. Set up a house for a needy family (refugee, single mom)

3. Go on a short-term mission trip

4. Help a missionary your church supports

5. Support those recovering from a natural disaster or tragedy.

An adventure such as these brings a deeper joy knowing that with your hands and your feet you can share love to others. While you serve, things happen. You talk, you disciple, you make bonds, and you learn to lead.

If going away for a long trip is not possible, look for something to do closer to home. Start a "Spy Kids on Mission" program. Invite kids and parents to serve the local community. Let the parents know where you're going, but let the kids be surprised to find out their "secret mission" for the day by solving a puzzle or clue. Here are some possible adventures:

- visit hospitals and bring cards, coloring books, and games
- visit nursing homes where you can read books and play games with the residents
- make blankets for teen moms
- put together kits for the homeless
- have canned food collections
- enhance a local shelter
- set up an apartment (for refugees or needy families)
- collect school supplies
- sort clothes for benevolence
- write letters to missionaries and build care packages for them
- make thank you baskets for nearby businesses
- bring baked goods to the fire or police department
- clean up a beach or park

OH, THE PLACES YOU'LL GO!

Final Thoughts

I'm so glad that we serve a big God who can do more than we can even imagine! I can't wait to see just where He will take you and His church! Of course, you can't do it all, but just take a step, as Dr. Seuss states,

> *"So be sure when you step,*
> *Step with care and great tact.*
> *And remember that life's*
> *A Great Balancing Act.*
> *And will you succeed?*
> *Yes! You will, indeed!*
> *(98 and 3/4 percent guaranteed.)*
> *KID, YOU'LL MOVE MOUNTAINS!"*

We can take it further when we partner with God. It is 100% guaranteed that God will use this next generation to bring Him glory as they discover which mountains He will help them move through their amazing ability to lead.

> *"Now to him who is able to do immeasurably more than all we ask or imagine, according to his power that is at work within us, to him be glory in the church and in Christ Jesus throughout all generations, for ever and ever! Amen"* Ephesians 3:20-21 (NIV).

Lisa Davis, the Children's Ministry Director of Alderwood Community Church in Lynnwood, WA, delights in telling stories and encouraging others to share the greatest story of all in such a way that kids and adults are captivated by the beauty and love of Jesus. Her family of 6 loves living in the great Northwest and enjoys camping, the ocean, and hiking.

chapter 17

FARTS, FELLOWSHIP, AND FRIENDSHIPS

Engaging Boys and Loving It

BY RICHARD WEEKS

CREATING OPPORTUNITIES for preteen boys to make good friends at church, while teaching them to grow spiritually is no easy task for a teacher. Boys have a tendency to smell bad, move a lot, and make a lot of noise. Embracing and appreciating their "messiness" while establishing clear boundaries for accepted behaviors in class creates the environment where great things happen in small chunks of time.

SET THE STAGE

My overall goal with a group of fourth to sixth grade boys is to create an environment where they make good friends and learn about Jesus. It requires flexibility along with the ability to know what matters most, so true growth and learning happens. Kids need an adult to set the stage, showing them the value of creating an environment with acceptance, encouragement, help, and mutual respect. I consider the class a small group and my role as the teacher is to help them grow into their position as equal members of the group, collaborating on common goals, learning how to love each other in spite of our personalities or habits, and accomplishing something big together.

We often start class with a sign-in notebook that allows for capturing names, birthdays, grades, or whatever we want. Gathering information this way allows us to celebrate special days and provides an informal way for the boys to learn about each other as the notebook is passed around. Creativity is encouraged and graffiti such as drawings, jokes, or nicknames are often added. We also use the notebook to allow them to select a number from a range (e.g. between 1-25). The teacher reveals the winning number at the end of class and the winner chooses candy from our candy bucket or at times, a handful of candy. We keep the drawing to the end because the class knows it is dependent on us working together to achieve what we are trying to do that class to have the time for a winner.

Making time for an icebreaker is important (and it's important to explain what the term means, I discovered). Choose one that is both fun and revealing. Icebreakers serve multiple purposes. They allow everyone a chance to talk in a structured, easy manner. They allow everyone the chance to practice listening—giving another their full attention, leading to a deeper understanding of mutual respect.

Icebreakers also provide opportunities to discover common experiences, likes and dislikes. Doing an icebreaker each time you meet allows kids to practice these skills repeatedly. All this rolls into the desire to create that environment where all are making friends and learning about Jesus. A fun one for boys: Tell us about one of your scars and how you got it.

FAMILIES

It's important to recognize the variety of family situations to avoid excluding kids. Some kids are in divorced homes and have two sets of families, so they only come to church every other week. Others live with other family members, and maybe a grandparent or aunt/uncle brings them to church. Many kids have a mom or dad in prison, and some come from homes with same-sex parents. Be careful with your words because of these differences. You can easily cause a feeling of separation if your viewpoint is coming from a "normal" mom and dad family that comes to church together. I try not to make a big deal about any of the family relationships, but accept the make-up as reality, just as the kids do. It's their life and it's normal to them, so be willing to be uncomfortable sometimes when you don't have the personal experience to relate. Go ahead and feel awkward, for their sakes. Don't be afraid to ask questions like, "Did you get to visit your dad in prison this month?" or "What's it like moving from your mom's house to your dad's house every other week?"

IT'S OKAY IF YOU DON'T FINISH THE LESSON

Always be ready with your lesson. Make sure you've designed it to allow time for questions and explanations. Be sure your lesson is at their level, based on what you know about their lives, their reading levels, and spiritual growth. Teaching through a gospel is a great method for this age group. They probably have a Bible at home so they can read what was studied and for those kids who only come every other week, it's not hard to catch up. So much Jesus and so many tough sayings to explore together.

An environment that encourages wrong answers and guesses will help your boys learn. Ask them what they know. Let them teach each other. Correct them if they're off track. Stay mindful of words they may not yet know, such as leprosy, tabernacle, and all the names of people and places. Make the time to give the background so they can connect the dots. Finishing a lesson cannot be your primary goal; instead, make the primary goal the process of learning, of exploring God's Word in a safe place, and making progress with other guys.

BOUNDARIES

John Townsend in his article called "Why Kids Need Boundaries" (focusonthefamily.com) lists four steps involved in setting boundaries—love, truth, freedom, and reality. He also notes three results that kids with boundaries learn—a sense of self, self-control, and great relationships. These results line up with my vision for a class of boys.

In our classes, boundaries are set using simple ideas such as treat others with respect, listen when it's not your turn to speak, and raise your hand to answer a question. You must know what your expectations are and the students must too. If you're unsure of expectations, how can you have boundaries that can be used in class? The benefits of following these simple rules are explained, especially the importance of working together so we have a class that everyone else wants to be in.

Reminding someone of your expectations when they speak out of turn, pass gas, make fun of someone, or crack a less than appropriate joke can be a challenge. As Townsend mentions in his article, it is important to speak and act with unconditional love when dealing with boundaries. It's so important to allow them the opportunity to "save face"—to correct in love in a way that allows them to change the behavior by choice. Shutting a kid down with shame or force is a shortsighted solution. While it may resolve the immediate problem, it shows other students that there is a high price to pay for mistakes and easily shuts down the open environment needed for developing camaraderie and mutual encouragement.

Consequences for failing to follow class rules follow the structure we use in our elementary kidmin department.

In all transparency, there are times when I jump to threatening a strike four in frustration at a continuing behavior or one that is severely sidetracking the class. This prevents the student from "saving face" and puts me in the awkward position of having to roll back my threat, apologize, and rethink what I need to do to guide us back on track. It's so important to avoid resorting to threats or using a "sledgehammer to kill a gnat." It helps build and maintain credibility and mutual respect, and adds to the goal of creating an environment where they make friends and learn about Jesus.

RELATIONSHIPS

Developing relationships with your class of boys takes great effort on the teacher's part. You must learn about their hobbies, what sports they like and are involved in, and how their school life goes. Engage them in conversation—ask them about life—and then really listen to what they say. Teach them their value by showing that you value them. Make time to praise them to their parents (or whoever picks them up from class) in front of them. Whether success was great or small, let them see how much they are valued and how they contribute to the success of the class.

Time spent building relationships is well spent—resulting in effective classroom management. Mutual respect is earned and developed. Make opportunities to teach respect, reward them for successes, and have fun while doing it. Use adult leaders who are consistently there so this growth can occur. You need teachers who love these boys and are willing to accept the responsibility for creating the environment needed for building friendships and learning about Jesus. You need men who are willing to take risks and reveal appropriate facts of their own lives and who will own their mistakes when their words or actions don't live up to the class expectations. These other adult leaders must be mentored and provided opportunities to take active roles in the classroom. Their gifts will add to the overall growth in the class; don't depend solely on a primary teacher. The same opportunities to establish mutual respect and provide loving discipline are needed so their role is clear to the students.

An invaluable activity we are able to do is periodically pull students into the hall for one-on-one time. We meet in the hall because it is very public and sit right in front of a window and security camera. We don't put any child in danger being off alone with a leader. While another leader teaches a lesson inside the classroom, we meet to talk about life. This time is all about the student and they get my full attention. I take notes and let them know I'll share with the other leaders with their permission so we can all be in prayer and agreement for the things they are working on. This also gives us the ability to follow up and check their progress as our paths continue to cross. We can talk about anything they like, but I have some common topics that are good to cover such as family relationships, friends at school, are they leaders or followers, and influence. Additionally, we talk about their general goals and specifically their spiritual goals— how often are they reading the Bible, what is their prayer time like, and have they talked about Jesus with anyone. I usually let them pick who comes out next, as part of the fun. Besides the obvious benefits of having an adult give them full attention and care about their lives, I've seen some of the most reserved and passive boys change into very active participants in class after just one of these talks.

After months together, building the sense of community and belonging, we sponsor all-boy events to add to that sense of being part of something cool. We also host fishing events that involve some of the boys' dads. Many times, it's someone's first time to go fishing or to catch a fish. It's wonderful to see the competitive nature of our boys being tempered with collaboration, encouragement, and celebration as they learn to bait hooks, cast lines, and catch fish.

WORSHIP AND PRAYER

We use a large group/small group format in our kidmin area. Developing a safe environment in the small groups leads to opportunities for boys to worship and pray in front of each other. Our role as teachers is to create opportunities for them to practice these types of God-focused disciplines. When the environment is created where practice is okay, not being perfect at something is encouraged, and trying something new is applauded, boys are freer to try things that will otherwise embarrass them. They need opportunities to check in with the rest of the boys about something praiseworthy in their lives—how God has come through for them and their family, praying for others aloud during class, using God's Word to declare victory over problems, or singing a song to the Lord. These opportunities must be planned so there is time for them to happen, instruction on what they are, and why they are important. Demonstrating how to do things and allowing time for practice, challenge, and refinement are all part of the process.

One example of this was a prayer night we had in class. Needs were written on note pads and then the boys and leaders took them to different locations in the room. The only requirements were that we not interfere with each other and that we behaved in a respectful way because of the importance of what we were about to do. Worshipful music was played while we each prayed in our own ways for the needs of the others. The music was in part to provide a "cover" so no one was concerned about anyone listening to what they were saying. They were encouraged to assume whatever position felt right to them that night—on their knees, laying down, eyes open or closed, and so on. We used time at the end of the evening to process how it went and the responses ranged from "When can we do it again?" to "That was kind of weird." That experience opened the doors to additional practice in praying and worshiping as a group and allowed us to try different techniques to see what "fit" us the best.

Involving families in this growth requires an education effort as well. You need to let them know what you are learning and doing and how they can encourage their boys. As we all know, sometimes kids are further along than their families and can many times be the reason a family is at church at all. Often, interactions with parents or guardians have to be squeezed in before and after class in the hallway to discuss special needs, pray, and talk about strategies for growth specific to the family's situation. Even these quick meetings are invaluable because they reinforce the value of the class and the importance of making it to church. It is also when I learn invaluable tidbits about the boys—challenges at school that were previously unknown, visits to see a parent in prison, medications being taken, family illnesses, and other highly impactful situations that are critical to ministry.

CONCLUSION

The temptation to make a group of preteen boys just sit still and be quiet so you can finish teaching a lesson has to be balanced with the reality that their lives may be complicated by family, school, or medical issues that are going to "leak out" into class. Let the goal of helping them to make good friends and learn about Jesus guide what happens in your class as you create situations where their rougher edges can be worked off—where they can learn they are not alone and that other guys also have struggles. Prioritize relationship building over any fixed need to "teach a lesson" or complete something in class. Instead, keep the primary goal the process of learning, exploring God's Word in a safe place, and making progress with other guys.

Richard Weeks is an ordained minister and a 2017 graduate of Christian Family Church International Bible Institute in San Antonio, TX. He serves together with his much better half, Trish Weeks, in New Braunfels, TX.

chapter 18

INVESTMENT OPPORTUNITY

Engaging Kids Through Small Groups

BY MICHAEL BOWEN

WE'VE ALL SEEN IT. The aftermath of children's ministry on any given day. The detritus of paper floating around the emptying parking lot. Yes, the "parking lot confetti" of those flyers and pamphlets that you spent your precious time painstakingly creating the perfect layout to communicate your message to the parents. You edited the content so that just the main topics of the message you share with the children can be reinforced at home. Where do they often end up? Rarely do they end up in the hands of the parents! How can we effectively work with the parent in their role of training up their children? How can the church minister to these little ones?

The small group leader is the one in the church who is in a strategic position to be able to impact the lives of individual students. Whether a little one or a youth, it's this position which can build a relationship that allows one to invest in the life of the young one. This integral role has the capacity to build disciples and train up to be the next generation who will work actively within the church. Consider the progression of faith passed down to the next generation found in 2 Timothy 1:5 (ESV), *"I am reminded of your sincere faith, a faith that dwelt first in your grandmother Lois and your mother Eunice and now, I am sure, dwells in you as well."* First and foremost, the responsibility belongs to the parent. It is the role of the Church to come alongside to equip and encourage the parent in this responsibility. The large group lessons are just as important in spiritual growth for the child as listening to the pastor's sermons are for adults. However, these lessons are one-directional instructions that are not disciple-making opportunities.

Why the focus on discipleship? Without this focus, the church may as well be just another daycare service. Yes, the Bible may be taught, and good lessons routinely enforced, but a public school will also teach good morals and good citizenship lessons. Discipleship aims to do more than simply teach good living; it teaches how to impact this world with the Gospel for eternity. It teaches how to view things through an eternal mindset and to *"seek the things that are above"* Colossians 3:1 (ESV). It seeks to teach the disciple to have the same attitude as Paul when he instructed Timothy, *"... and what you have heard from me in the presence of many witnesses entrust to faithful men who will be able to teach others also"* 2 Timothy 2:2 (ESV). These fall in line with the Great Commission which Jesus gave to His disciples before ascending to heaven. He didn't tell them to go make converts, or to build up great buildings. He told them to go and make disciples, baptizing and *"teaching them to observe all that I have commanded you"* Matthew 28:20 (ESV). Yes, baptize them into the faith, but it doesn't end there. If you were to stop at that point, you would not be observing this last commandment of Jesus to His disciples. You are to teach others to obey all that Jesus commanded. You are to make disciples.

Dr. Robert E. Coleman, in his book *The Master Plan of Evangelism,* points out that through Jesus' selection of a handful of men, He set out to evangelize the world. In other words, by working with a few, you can impact the many. Jesus invested time and energy into the lives of His disciples. He taught them, He modeled life for them, and He sent them out with specific instructions (Mark 6:7-13; Luke 9:1-6; Matthew 10). Jesus modeled a pattern that you should follow: invest in the lives of a few that they may broaden an overall reach through a pattern of multiplication. Jesus turned His disciples into disciple-makers and then told them to do the same with others. It has been through this pattern, passed down through the centuries, that you have the message of the cross today.

The role of the small group leader is nothing close to the role of babysitter. No, their role is to invest in the lives of their small group. They should see their ministry as an opportunity to build disciples who will one day train their own. After all, that is the role of the disciple-maker: a ministry of multiplication. The challenge the Church faces is to equip these disciple-makers to invest in their disciples. Such an in-depth task cannot be fully accomplished within the one or two hours often assigned to children's and youth ministries. The small group setting is an opportune place to begin this process. But, how is one to accomplish this enormous feat in ministry today?

Consistency is one key term to remember. Whatever ministry tool your church decides to use, it is important to be as consistent as possible with the same small group participants. As much as is possible, determine to have the same members each week so that you can build trusting relationships with the disciples. This established trust opens opportunity to minister in life-changing possibilities. It allows for natural, heart-deep conversations to develop which may take weeks to complete. The personal nature of these conversational rhythms is only possible through an established relational trust. Chances are, if you reflect upon an adult (other than a parent) who made an impact in your life as a child, they will be someone who had a consistent, personal investment in your life.

In ministry, it is also important to be consistent in showing up to be involved. Establishing permanent small groups without a consistent small group leader undermines the entire process. It's not just the role of the children's ministers or other church staff (paid or unpaid) to be committed to this work! Too often the church body is content to let the staff do it because it is viewed as "their job." They may get paid to do the work, but the work belongs to all members of the body of Christ! Failure to step up to the role and come alongside the staff is failure to be invested in the role God has called His Church to fulfill.

Whether it is in children's or youth ministries or any other activity of the church, the entire body is responsible to be active in service. The staff can only lead and guide others in the work. The others must be consistent in being available to invest in the lives of the students. If you are consistent, then challenge others to be as well. Sometimes, a peer is more effective in encouragement to consistency than one in a leadership role. The greatest thing to remember is that this is a ministry opportunity! Regardless of the ministerial tool you use, it is an evangelistic opportunity to make disciples of the next generation. If this is an important task, then you, as a church leader, must commit yourself wholly to accomplishing it!

While being present is very important, you need to be active while there. One who is there to fulfill a role but spends the time talking with friends and catching up on their lives without spending time investing in the students is not being useful in the work. While there to do the work, do not become distracted by extraneous things which reduce your ministerial impact.

Consistency is the first responsibility, and being involved is the next. One of the best ways to encourage students to engage in an activity is to model that engagement yourself! By setting an example, you model the intended result. Jesus taught the masses, He healed the sick, and then He sent His disciples to do the same. It is important that a small group leader is engaged in the material with which they are working. If you're working through a Bible study, read the passage and answer the questions yourself prior to coming to be with the kids. Do not let the first time you see the material be in front of the students. Be prepared so that you can be an effective role model and an effective teacher.

Being involved doesn't only mean being prepared. It also means investing in the lives of your small group. Take the time to get to know them, to know their interests. Do they play on a sports team? Make an effort to go to one of their games. Do they have a role in the school play? Take a group to go watch it. Did they have a major event happen in their family? Invest in their life by showing that you are aware of it and that you care. Take the time to communicate with them outside of scheduled activities; the result will be an increased relational awareness between those involved. They will be more Christ-like in their lives when you show them that you care for them in a Christ-like manner. You will model what a disciple of Christ looks like so that they can be more like Christ.

To be an effective disciple-maker in a small group setting requires both consistency and involvement. This involvement leads to the necessity of following up on commitments and challenges. Being dependable is another important trait of the leader. This does tie into the first two qualities but is still distinct enough to warrant its own attention. Dependability will increase the value of the relationships that you establish with the students. If you commit to doing everything and follow through with nothing, then your word also means nothing. If you say that you're going to do something, then be faithful and do what you said. In Matthew 21:28-32, Jesus tells the parable about two sons who are told to work in the vineyard. One says he will but does not do any work. The other son says no, but reconsiders and eventually does the work he initially rejected. Jesus' focus here is on the action: the son who actually did the work is the one who did what his father wanted. In the same way, when you say that you will do something but refuse to take the action of that commitment, you lower your dependability in the eyes of those you disappoint. If you're not dependable in what you say, why should you be believable in what you say in small group time? Your actions often speak louder than your words.

You can be consistent, involved, and follow through in all your commitments, but you must remember that you are not in this alone. You must always remember to stop and pray for your small group. If you've taken the time to get to know each one individually, you will notice needs that beg for intercession. You're in a position to stand alongside them through prayer. Ask for prayer requests, write them down, and then pray for these requests. Keep a journal through the year which will allow you to continue to pray for their needs and remind you to ask them about their situations. This will increase your investment in their lives and show them another way that you care for them.

While you need to pray for the students, you also should pray with them. Model prayer for them so they can see how a mature Christian prays. Teach them to pray by encouraging them to participate in the prayer time. Don't forget that prayer is not only requesting things of God, but also praising Him for His blessings, worshipping Him for His character, and giving glory to God in general. Teach the practical methods of prayer, but also the faith that comes with talking to God. Remind them of the special privilege that you have to bring your requests directly to Him. Show that you don't need lengthy prayers, but quick prayers work well when you don't know what to say. Reveal to them that even Jesus took time out of His busy schedule to spend time with His Father.

The challenge to be involved in the lives of these young disciples and to impact their lives in an eternal way is a tremendous task. Yet, it is something that Jesus challenged His disciples to do and then to pass on to others. This challenge has been passed down to you and you must implement, execute, and accomplish this same task with those you disciple. Jesus worked to impact this world by investing in the lives of a small group of men. The small group leader is walking the same path.

As a husband, father, and faith-supported missionary with Global Children's Network, **Michael Bowen** is passionate about developing leaders in the multiplying ministry of disciple making. He speaks in churches, camps, Bible colleges, and conferences equipping pastors, ministry leaders, and parents around the world and across denominations.

chapter 19

NO MONOLOGUES ALLOWED!
Engaging Kids from the Stage

BY CORINNE NOBLE

WHETHER YOU'VE BEEN in kids' ministry for a while or just a few weeks, you've probably noticed that a lot is required out of leaders when it comes to engaging the audience—kids. You have to be good communicators in one-on-one situations, in small groups, and on the stage. Most of you probably gravitate towards being one or the other. I've always preferred large group communicating from a stage, and I've really had to work hard at becoming comfortable in a small group setting. It's highly important that you learn to become good communicators in both settings. For the next few pages I'll be focusing on how to effectively communicate and engage kids from a stage in a large group setting. Now, some of you may have an actual, physical stage in your kids' ministry environments, and others might not. If you don't, that's okay! You don't need to have a physical stage for the tips to be applicable to your ministry. When I use the term "stage" it is considered the front of the room, or the area from which you teach in a large group setting.

IT TAKES A TEAM

Speaking of stage teams, you need one! You might be starting off with "me, myself, and I," and many of you have been there, but you can't stay in a singular state forever. You're bound to burn yourself out being a one man/woman show, and the kids will likely get bored of hearing the same person all the time. You need to start raising up and training a team of diverse leaders to tag-team the large group elements of your service. Nothing makes me more thankful for my team than when I have to do an entire service by myself. It is exhausting! It may seem like pulling teeth to train your leaders on how to effectively communicate with the kids from the stage, but you'll be so glad you did.

ENTER WITH A BANG

When you enter the stage, bring the energy level you want to see from the kids. You can't come out on the stage with your energy level low and expect the kids to wake you up. The leaders on the stage set the energy level for the room. I've heard leaders complain about how the kids are "dead" or have no energy, especially in a service that's earlier in the day. I've found that if you keep bringing the higher energy level on the stage, the kids' energy level will rise to meet yours.

Before you begin explaining the service element you're leading, always introduce yourself by telling the kids your name and position. For example: "Hey guys! I'm Pastor Corinne and I'm so excited to share today's game with you." You should always think about stage communication from the perspective of a guest or newer kids who have no idea who you are or what's going on. Introducing yourself also adds a personal element to an otherwise impersonal moment. Take this concept to the next level by making an effort to learn the kids' names and use them when you're calling on them. Have you ever seen a kid's face light up when you use their name? It only takes small gestures like knowing a kid's name to have a huge impact.

Know what you're planning on doing or saying before you get on the stage. Some people may be more comfortable with "winging it" than others, but the kids can tell when you have absolutely no idea what's going on. If you're distracted because you are under-prepared or holding a piece of paper in your hand, it will be nearly impossible for you to effectively engage the kids. It's also important to know what's coming up next on the schedule and who's leading it. Sometimes that person is in the bathroom, home sick, putting a Bandaid on a kid's finger, or they weren't paying attention. If you're leading on the stage, it is your responsibility to keep the service going and engage the kids. This can be a bigger issue as your stage team becomes larger and includes more leaders.

If you have access to microphones in your ministry, use them! This may seem like common sense, but I've met some leaders who have a phobia of holding a microphone. If you're in a large room with more than 10 children, a microphone is a resource you need to keep control of your audience. Always speak into the microphone if you're on the stage. If you call on a kid or use volunteers during your service, allow them to speak in the microphone as well. It is impossible to engage the entire audience if they can't hear what's going on.

MAKE IT INTERACTIVE

The title of this chapter is "No Monologues Allowed" for a reason. If you just stand on a stage and talk at the children for an hour, you'll lose the majority of their attention. Not only will they not be engaged in what you're teaching, but they'll likely leave your services having learned nothing new, because they checked out in the first five minutes. You always want to keep the kids' attention so you can teach them something new and exciting about God's Word.

Kids love questions! Ask lots of questions during every stage element to confirm the kids are still listening. Questions can be for the whole audience requiring an action in response. For example, "Jump up out of your chair if you know last week's memory verse." Questions can also allow individual kids to have the opportunity to contribute to the learning experience. For example, ask, "Who can remind us of the five books of the Bible we learned about last week?" Sometimes, these opportunities to interact can cause kids' answers to derail your service and send you down an unwanted bunny trail with their lengthy stories. The stage leader should always know when and how to nicely and swiftly shut down an answer that's getting off track.

If you feel like you're losing the kids' attention, you can always re-engage them with a repeat-after-me statement. You can use this technique with just about anything. For example, during announcements, you can have the kids repeat the date of an event, or during the message, you can have the kids repeat the main character's name every time you say it. Take it to the next level by getting kids out of their seats and adding motions to a repeat-after-me statement. This will engage multiple senses and get everyone to refocus on what is happening on the stage.

Any time you're using the Bible, make it interactive! Get the kids involved and engaged in God's Word individually. You might be thinking, "Most of my kids forget their Bibles at home and never bring them to church." I have definitely experienced this frustrating problem, but my team came up with a great solution! We purchased some affordable Bibles in a translation that is kid-friendly (we prefer NIV and NLT) and created the Bible Bin. The Bible Bin is quite literally a bin full of Bibles that we provide for the kids to borrow during the service if they forgot their Bibles. We still encourage the kids to bring their own Bibles, and if a kid doesn't own a Bible at all, we will give them a brand new Bible to take home. Once you have your own Bible Bin in place, there is no excuse for any of the kids to be disengaged during the message or any other time you're using a Bible during the service. You can even do an old-fashioned sword drill and have the kids race to find the weekly memory verse. Before beginning the message, you should always tell the kids the passage in the Bible and allow time for them to turn to the passage with you before continuing on with the message. It is so important to use the Bible from the stage and have the kids individually dig into it with you every week.

Team and individual incentives/competitions are great ways to engage kids from the stage. We've done boys vs. girls, colors, and grades. I've found that seating the kids by their ages or grades is the best way to engage them and helps them form relationships with kids their own age. You can offer points, bucks, candy, or prizes to individuals or teams that are participating. Following the rules/expectations, and answering questions about what they have been taught are great ways to earn incentives. Switch up your incentives and competitions to keep the kids excited and interested in achieving their goals.

Know how to read your audience from the stage. Are the kids bored, talking, fidgeting, moving around, misbehaving, or constantly asking to go to the bathroom? It may be time to wrap up whatever you're doing or change your method to get more time out of their attention spans. You can change up your method of teaching by showing a video clip, playing a game, or doing an object lesson. Every time you switch up your method, you will re-engage the kids' attention.

TRICKY TRANSITIONS

Transitions are so small and seemingly harmless, but they can be super tricky to master. Again, the more people there are on your stage team, the trickier it will be to nail your transitions. A good rule of thumb is that the stage should never be "dead." A dead stage means that no one is on the stage, no one is speaking, and there is not a video playing. It only takes about

5 seconds of dead stage time to lose the kids' attention. A leader should always be walking on the stage immediately after another leader leaves the stage. If the next leader is not ready to go, the leader who is on the stage should stall by lengthening the current service item or move on to the next scheduled item without them. Quick and seamless transitions are essential. Use video bumpers to make transitions easier for your stage team and keep the stage from becoming dead during a transition.

PREPARE, PREPARE, PREPARE

I know you and your stage team are busy. Everyone's heard the excuses for why a volunteer hasn't looked at the service schedule until the moment they walked on the stage. I have a rule for myself and my stage team that I stick to: You should never be holding a schedule or curriculum in your hand on the stage. This might seem like an impossible rule for you to enforce, but you'll see a huge difference in how your stage team engages with the kids when their faces aren't buried in a sheet of paper.

There are some ways to cheat on this without losing engagement with the kids. You can use a confidence monitor or screen in the back of the room to help with knowing what to say or what's up next. You can use a cart or stand on the stage for messages and have your notes on the stand. Resist the urge to hide behind the cart and have your eyes glued to your notes! You can hold a Bible in your hand and read from it. Sneak a cheat sheet in your Bible with your outline and mark your scriptures to find them quickly. I always remind my leaders that it's more important to connect with the kids and make eye contact with them, than to say everything exactly as it is written on the page.

CONNECT WITH KIDS OFFSTAGE

If you really want to engage the kids on the stage, a good place to start is building relationships with the kids offstage. If a leader is not on the stage, they should always be sitting with kids, participating, worshipping, and interacting with them. Leaders should not be hanging out in the back of the room or chatting with other leaders during service. I have no idea why leaders always seem to gravitate towards standing or sitting in the back of the room unless you train them to do otherwise. You can't lead from behind! Zig Ziglar said, "People don't care how much you know until they know how much you care." When you show the kids that you are genuinely interested in spending time with them and hearing about their lives off the stage, they will be more likely to listen to you when you're speaking to them on the stage.

We are by no means running a perfect kids' service, but we're always working towards a higher level of excellence, because our kids deserve it and God has entrusted us with teaching them.

Corinne Noble is a Children's Pastor at Desert Springs Church in Chandler, AZ. She received her call to kids' ministry when she was only ten years old, and has been involved in it ever since. She enjoys writing curriculum, creating set designs, and sharing her ideas with other kids' ministry leaders. When she's not doing ministry, she loves to cook, bake, and spend time with her husband, Sean.

chapter 20

AS CLOSE AS YOUR BACK YARD
Engaging Kids in International Missions

BY KENDRA JOYNER

A S I BEGIN TO THINK about the honor and privilege it is to engage kids in international missions it brings me back to my own very first international mission trip. The very first part of being trained and prepared to go on a mission trip was learning to share my story. Sharing my story of who I was before Christ, after I accepted Christ, and what He was doing in my life currently! Learning to share the Gospel with those around me in a conversation was such a blessing and privilege; I was grateful for intentional training. It changed the way I even thought of missions and other people. If I didn't have a heart to share the greatest gift with those the Lord placed in my path, then I had no business going anywhere ... not even next door.

I thought we would travel the world, but little did I know the world was right at my doorstep. I had a wonderful missionally-minded church that wanted to reach every tribe, nation, and tongue even right on our doorsteps. One of the best ways to engage kids and their families in missions is to begin right where you are.

It's amazing at what a melting pot we have in our own back yards. I grew up in a military town that also hosted migrant workers to bring in tomato crops each summer. With that being said, my home church hosted a migrant Vacation Bible School for families who moved around every two weeks or so to the next location. We not only fed them a meal, we fed them spiritually for two weeks with teaching them the Word of God that does not return void. We also prepared bags for them called health kits that had a towel, a Bible, a bar of soap, shampoo, toothpaste, toothbrush, and a comb or brush as well as a few pieces of American candy. We gave out the health kits to anyone who attended on Thursday evening of Vacation Bible School. We needed to meet physical and spiritual needs as we invested in each of their lives for the short time we had contact with them.

I remember helping lead a fourth grade class with my mother who taught the Bible lesson each night. I was just in fifth grade myself but she gave me the job of not only making our new friends feel welcome but teaching them a game to take with them to their new destination. Now the game was not just a fun game, it had to be a game that encouraged and backed up the Bible lesson as well.

You must remember kids can sometimes reach other kids in a completely different way than adults can. Don't hesitate to let the children in your body of Christ learn to lead others even when it comes to other nationalities. 1 Timothy 4:12 (ESV) reminds us, *"Let no one despise you for your youth, but set the believers an example in speech, in conduct, in love, in faith, in purity."* Children have a very teachable, moldable spirit and international missions is a great place to start.

Children have opportunities in school each day to engage in international missions as they sit next to a classmate who could be from another country and has relocated to the United States. Give encouragement to your families and friends to befriend those new students. With our influx of refugee families all around the United States, what a great way to engage in international missions right where you are! You can also encourage your families to be a part of community outreach opportunities such as coat drives, community sports events, community wide festivities, or food pantries. Learn as a family how to greet those new refugees coming into our country to make this their home. We have a World Relief office nearby in our community and our opportunities to reach families and give rides to church is a huge opportunity for us.

We know that ministry is messy, but we could not imagine what blessings the Lord gives us as we are faithful to the ministry He calls us to. These sweet families have not even seen a light switch before or had indoor plumbing or a couch to sit on. So, it's important that we take time to engage and teach them about their new surroundings. Just as we go through culture shock when we visit other countries and are feeling out of place, the same is true for our new friends and refugee families who join us here in the United States. Don't be afraid to take the opportunities the Lord gives you in your own community. Join Him at work right there!

While attending a disciple-making conference not long ago, one of the take-aways I came home with is that we can engage our brothers and sisters from other countries, but many times they want to show us hospitality into their culture and not expect us to just fix the needs that they may have. How many times do you have a refugee family or a family from your community who is different, invite you in for tea or dinner? That's a great way for your children and families to engage in international missions.

I would also say, that engaging kids in international missions comes in all shapes and sizes wherever the Lord places you. As your family travels for vacations, meeting a neighbor or new friend in your community, or even intentional mission trips, show your children what the similarities and differences are for other people and the importance of sharing the Gospel with all people. *"Therefore go and make disciples of all nations, baptizing them in the name of the Father and of the Son and of the Holy Spirit, and teaching them to obey everything I have commanded you. And surely I am with you always, to the very end of the age."* Matthew 28:19-20 (NIV). The kingdom of God will contain every tribe, nation, and tongue. Children are able to grasp that concept much more than many adults. Let their sense of adventure engage them in a great adventure of international missions.

Don't be hesitant to connect with those who are already doing international missions as a family! They are able to give great personal experience as to how they are living it out in an international setting and also encourage those who are interested in joining in where they are. Don't be hesitant to go and share in international missions on many different levels with your children and families. Some ways we encourage our kids and expose them to international missions is we intentionally use a portion of our summer to Skype with families who are currently serving on the mission field that have been a part of our church.

That way, our kids can ask about their living situations and how they are learning new things where their home is now. We had children ask a few of these questions last summer. How do you meet other children in your neighborhood? What kind of shoes do you wear where you currently live? Where do you get water from? How many times do you take a bath a week? How do you learn the language in the town that you live in? Where is the nearest church and what does it look like? Is church similar or different from what you experienced here in the United States? We wanted to encourage children to explore and ask questions but also remember that because there are some differences of time, safety, and security, we could not answer some of their questions.

Don't be afraid to allow children to engage and learn hands-on at home before taking a trip to another country. The Lord has created a beautiful world around you and it is wonderful to see Him at work in and around you in His world for His good and His glory! What an opportunity with a wide open world to engage in international missions.

We have all been commanded to go and make disciples of all nations. If you're looking for opportunities to travel intentionally on an international mission trip, I would say, go as a family or church family. Serve together, learn together, share together as a family. Children are able to connect with other children immediately! It is also a unique opportunity for you to experience with your family a precious time of sharing the Gospel and serving others in another cultural context. It doesn't necessarily have to begin with a non-English speaking country if that thought scares you. There are many other English-speaking countries that need others to come to share the love of Christ and the truth of the Gospel with them. We also have countries that are included as international countries that aren't far from home, that you could embark to in order to share Christ and serve in international missions.

The Lord allows each of us to have different gifts and talents to share with the world. One of the many talents and gifts that children are able to share anywhere is a smile that portrays the love of Christ. We also are able to allow children to learn new games and songs because both of those things speak through cultural and language barriers. I would encourage you to be adventuresome with your children and allow them to experience other cultures and opportunities to share the Gospel in whatever door the Lord opens in whatever country.

While cultural differences may affect children when they visit other countries, that can also be a barrier if you allow it to be in your own neighborhood. Thankfully, most children I've met are still moldable and curious when they see differences arise. It helps to take time to explain and talk about what they're seeing so they know how to process and be used in a flexible setting. One of the biggest keys I've learned when leading other teams in international missions is to remind them moment by moment to be flexible. The United States seems to be the only part of the world where time is such a concern. Many countries are not stuck on a schedule but allow relationships, people, and experiences to matter more than time does. Teach your children who are interested in international missions that time and schedule don't matter as much as the experience and relationships being built. While serving on a team it takes time to get a team to move from one location to another, but building relationships is by far a gift the Lord gives when traveling and serving in another country. In our age of technology, keeping in touch with those precious relationships is far easier today than ever before.

I would encourage you to give international missions an opportunity with the families and children in your ministry. All children have the ability to connect, serve, go, and give to those of other cultures. The Lord has commanded each of us to do so as you go and make disciples of all nations, no matter what part of the world or neighborhood you may find yourself. Simply be willing to go and engage with those the Lord places in your path for His good and His glory! The Scripture says, *"Everyone who believes in him will not be put to shame. For there is no distinction between Jew and Greek; for the same Lord is Lord of all, bestowing his riches on all who call on him. For everyone who calls on the name of the Lord will be saved. How then will they call on him in whom they have not believed? And how are they to believe in him of whom they have never heard? And how are they to hear without someone preaching? And how are they to preach unless they are sent? As it is written, 'How beautiful are the feet of those who preach the good news!'"* Romans 10:11-15 (ESV).

International missions is always an adventure and the Lord will give fruit in His time so be ready to plant those seeds and harvest them for His kingdom. Children are ready to go and be the beautiful feet of Christ in their neighborhood, school, church, community, or to another country when given the right opportunities and support from those around them! Let's engage kids to be on mission as the hands and feet of Christ!

Kendra Joyner is a children's and family minister in High Point, NC who has a love for engaging families in ministry and missions. She has been faithfully serving in children's ministry for 13 plus years!

chapter 21

TOT TIME BRAIN TRAIN
Engaging the Littlest Ones

BY KAREN APPLE

PICTURE THE ADORABLE FACE of a little one in your ministry. If this child could talk, he would say, "My brain is growing faster than yours. Oh yeah!" It's true! In the first three years, little learners form one million neuron connections per second and learn more than in any other 3-year period of life. They are learning at a rate never before understood, according to a Harvard study.

Each child has "wheels" that turn constantly, so get on board the "brain train" and engage your little ones in a learning adventure from the moment they arrive. Every time you smile, rock, play, sing, or read, you can demonstrate the likeness of their loving Shepherd, Jesus. It starts them on a faith journey that leads them to Jesus, God's one and only Son.

Call the nursery by its true ministry. It's a place where little ones learn, grow, and experience the love of Jesus. Parents thrill at the idea of loving care wrapped in a Jesus learning adventure. Volunteers step it up if they know their presence brings value and meaning. A department name can bring clarity. Post it. Say it often. Explain it. Expect everyone to live up to it. Example: TOT Time (Teaching Our Treasures) means teaching our little ones who their treasure is, as well as Teaching the Treasures from God's Word.

You are more than a babysitter. You do so much more than talk to the lady in the next rocker or stand, blending into the wallpaper. We are "Edu-Huggers" who demonstrate the heart and the hands of Jesus in every situation. So don't just grab any old lady off the shelf. Attract young and older workers who love little learners and will make the kids their primary focus ... folks who will board the Tot Time Brain Train as active participants, engaging little learners eye-to-eye and heart-to-heart.

Personal connections and learning adventures begin at the door. The edu-hugger who greets parents and children by name sets the tone for healthy relationships. There are few things as engaging as eye-to-eye twinkles and arms spread wide to embrace a little cutie. Parents find comfort, and babes are drawn in by love.

Edu-huggers know the children and call them by name. Brain studies indicate that your name is the first word you recognize as infants. This means when you say or sing the name of a little learner, you instantly connect with her. The classroom should resound with the name of each child. Use a child's name in a welcome poem that is the same each time she arrives. My name and a consistent routine speak comfort, stability, home. This is where I belong!

Good morning, Ella. I'm glad to see you.
Good morning, Ella. Jesus loves you.

Connect the child's name to the name and the love of Jesus while you rock, jiggle-walk, diaper, and play.

Henry, Henry, I love you.
Henry, Jesus loves you, too.
Henry, Henry, I love you
And Jesus loves you, too!

You can teach about Jesus all through the hour (or two).

Though it's a good idea for leaders to build relationships and engage kids on the floor where they play, an edu-hugger who is unable to get on the floor can be a wonderful asset as she (or he) rocks and jiggle-walks. The rocking chair is the perfect place for a loving leader to read, sing, comfort, and pray a blessing over a child. A consistent, written blessing gives leaders the confidence to say it and parents can use the same blessing at home until they are comfortable enough to write their own.

Dear Heavenly Father,
Wrap Samuel in your loving care and grace
All the days of His life.
Bless Him with the joy of knowing You.

Infants and toddlers often need to be comforted and calmed. It's a time to draw a finger across a child's brow while whispering, "You are loved, you are loved. Mrs. Apple (your name) loves you. Jesus loves you. You are loved." Comfort also comes through distraction. Hold the child as you jiggle-walk around the room pointing out the birds, butterflies, and flowers painted on the walls. Or stand at the window pointing to the beauty outside. Add a little poem to make the experience wondrous. Change the word "chipmunk" to something you see.

Who made the chipmunk, the bugs, and the bees?

Who made the birdies way up in the trees?

God made the chipmunk, the birds, and the bees!

God made the birdies way up in the trees!

Teaching opportunities abound during regular routines. At the diapering station, post pictures of animals for leaders to talk about and a Bible verse to say while each child is diapered. The verse will be heard by everyone each time a child visits the changing station. One church posted the verse: "Jesus said, 'Let the little children come to me,'" Luke 18:16. Then they added, "Jesus loves <u>Charlie</u>! Yay!"

A kidmin pastor who uses this verse told me about a restroom incident in a small church. One morning a 2-year-old, who no longer wore diapers, asked to be taken to the "big girl potty." The edu-hugger went with her to the ladies' room with three stalls. As she held the stall door closed, she heard the little girl say, "Jesus said, 'Let the little children come to me' Luke 18:16. Jesus loves Katie, YAY!" The leader could hardly control her laughter as she swung wide the door for the child to proudly walk out. Some memory verses will forever accompany the routine.

The clean-up routine is usually delayed until parents leave the worship service. This regular activity can be a learning experience for crawlers, toddlers, walkers, and runners. Add a little poem to bring joy to the mundane.

Toys away. Don't delay.
Help your leader have a happy day!
Jason is a good helper, good helper, good helper!
Jason is a good helper. Here is your high five!

Little babies are not ready for the routine of snack time, but as soon as kiddos can sit for just a couple of minutes, you can add it to your schedule. It's a learning experience that teaches control (waiting), social interaction, and a grateful heart. Again, a song captures their attention before you pray. It gives instructions and engages their hearts.

Come sit at the table with me, with me.
Come sit at the table with me.

Be very quiet. We're talking to God.
He listens to hear what we say.

Play is a fun part of a child's regular routine. Little ones are drawn in when WE play. My heart sparkles every time I walk into a Tot Time room where leaders sit on the floor playing WITH tiny tots. A few months ago, I entered a toddler room where Maddie was crying and wildly riding a blue rocking horse. I sat beside her and sang a silly, made-up-on-the-spot song that included her name. She stopped crying and each time I stopped singing, she said a few words from the song as a signal to sing it again. She memorized it after just a few repetitions. I was blown away at the thought of a simple message in a fun song was now planted in her memory. The song made us friends. Say the same poems. Sing the same songs. Add the child's name. Include the name of Jesus. Every week. Over and Over again.

A rocking horse, toys, and books are all teaching tools and the floor is a learning space for kids. It's their territory. Enter it with joy and join the playful fun the kids create.

Most of the toys were on the shelves. The drum that houses all the magical instruments sat hidden in the corner. The kids "read" books with leaders, opened and closed the kid-sized door of the playhouse repeatedly. But, where was Henry? A jingle sounded from the hidden corner. No words, just a jingle. I peeked to find Henry sitting, bottom down, inside the large drum with his legs hanging over its rim. Laughter signaled his delight at being found from the joyful sound of his jingle. Each child then played Henry's game of "hide and jingle." We added the words "I found Henry. I just LOVE Henry. JESUS loves Henry!" with a hug and finger on the tip of his nose.

Something a child is learning to do is the very thing he wants to do. While playing, notice something a child is doing. Show her how. Applaud when she succeeds. "You did it! You did it! Can you do it again?" Give encouragement and announce the deed. "Sally is helping the baby doll. You are so kind to feed the baby."

Crawlers and toddlers are learning to turn the pages of books. Cardboard books are best for their little fingers because their fine motor skills are still developing. Sit on the floor or in a rocker with a child in your lap and let THEM turn the pages. You can be sure you will never read all the words before a little hand turns the page. That's okay! Sometimes it's just, "Read one picture (not the words) and I will turn the page!" Let the child set the pace.

There will be times when you can tell a very short Bible story or sing a song to children one by one as you rock, jiggle-walk, or sit in their territory. But even little learners benefit from a corporate learning experience. My husband, Steve, and I taught the littles together for a couple of years. The eyes of kids lit up each time Steve went to the closet and, with a flourish, spread a quilt on the floor. At the same time, I gave the signal to sit, be still, and listen.

Come sit right here with me.
Come sit right here with me.
Let's sing a little song and listen.
Come sit right here with me.

We sat with them on the quilt, sang a song without accompaniment (because young kids learn the words to songs better without background music). We showed them our open Bible and told a brief Bible story. The ritual and specific order helped them know what to expect. It brought comfort, calm, and attention. Young learners are wired for order. Do it the same way and in the same order every time. This means you must post the order in which you do things for all edu-huggers to know. Equip leaders with the tools to be effective. Organize the room so each leader can find what they need.

I visit churches to observe children's ministries. One local church has an awesome Tot Time with an amazing Bible teacher, "Story Lady." She visits all the preschool classrooms, including the littles. This day, she arrived with all the tools she needed in hand. The edu-huggers sang a gather together song and placed each child in a seat embedded in the kidney shaped table. Story Lady knelt down in the curve of the table and put her hands together as a signal. All the edu-huggers knelt beside children and showed their praying hands. All the children listened as Story Lady thanked God for their snack.

While Story Lady laid out her treasures, the kids ate gold fish and drank from sippy cups. The gold fish crumbs were swept away as Story Lady began to teach. She said a poem about the Bible. Then she opened it and pointed to a page as she displayed it to the wide-eyed kids. She spoke of a little man who wanted to see Jesus. Jesus loved Zacchaeus and wanted to come home with him. The story was illustrated with small cardboard figures that the children could later touch and hold. "Jesus made YOU. Jesus loves YOU, and He wants to be YOUR friend forever," she said. The edu-huggers held a mirror in front of each child as Story Lady said, "Jesus loves _____" to each child when they saw their own image.

This sensitive, insightful teacher taught a complete lesson in just three minutes. She included the basics of early childhood faith formation:

Jesus MADE me
Jesus LOVES me
Jesus wants to be my FRIEND FOREVER. *(First Look, Think Orange)*

And the lesson application was very personal.

There is nothing more engaging than building relationships with our littlest learners. Make each child feel safe and cherished. Engage them during every routine. Play with them and talk to them, not to the lady in the next rocker. After all, their brains are on the Express Train. So ... get on board!

When you draw children in and lead each one to Jesus with a loving heart, your words, and your actions, you are shepherds and edu-huggers.

Karen Apple is an "edu-hugger," speaker, and coach who lives in North Carolina with her husband, Steve, the Apple of her eye. Kids, families, and kidmin leaders make her brain sparkle.

chapter 22

SMILE SCIENCE
Engaging Kids with a Smile

BY JENNIFER ESCALANTE

I N A WORLD FILLED WITH animated Emoji, a real live smile is priceless, and it's what kids are longing to see. It's what they really need. So how do you get your smile on?

Today's culture is enthralled with popular box office hits such as *The Emoji Movie* and *Inside Out.* By utilizing emoticons or animated characters to represent the emotions you feel, children and families are mesmerized by the connecting of their sense of belonging and purpose with their state of happiness through colourful, animated tales. In particular, the character Joy, in *Inside Out,* takes you on a journey from a happy, positive beginning that intersects with life's twists and traumas that alter her happiness and sense of security.

And this parallels with reality.

As the 21ˢᵗ century church endeavors to push beyond her four walls, your children's ministry will encounter more and more scenarios not worth smiling about as. You are sure to encounter more and more hurting children and families that are in need of a hope beyond their pain. Introducing Smile Science!

What is a smile? It is a beam of light streaming down from the Father of Lights reflecting through you, the crown of all of His creation. The innocence and fun-loving nature of every child is magnetized by the sparkle of a smile. The practicality of a smile warms the heart and causes the target audience to feel welcomed and loved.

"Every time you smile at someone, it is an action of love, a gift to that person, a beautiful thing." - Mother Teresa.

So in the science of a smile, how does it work? What causes a smile to be so impactful?

One contemporary insight on the neurological effects of a smile can be credited to Marco Iacoboni, a neuroscientist at the University of California in Los Angeles. He shares how your mirror neuron brain cells are activated by actions such as smiling in his new book, *Mirroring People: The Science of How We Connect to Others.* Iacoboni explains how he believes that when you interact with others, you use body language to communicate your feelings. You send social signals such as facial expressions, gestures, and postures as a way of communication. Mirror neuron brain cells seem to be expressly designed to unlock the feelings behind your body messages. These brain cells are quite essential in enhancing your social interactions with each other. Without mirror neurons, you would doubtfully experience the emotions of other individuals. The mirror neurons provide a kind of imitation of the facial expressions or body language you observe. This causes you to replicate the emotions they are associated with. So, when you receive the message of a smile, your "smile" mirror neurons are activated too! The neural activity stirs up the feelings connected with a smile. The natural response to this is a smile mirrored on your face!

God's design for you is to be a social being. The emotions and feelings you experience can connect you with the people you interact with! God wants to work through you for His purposes and His glory. *"For we are his workmanship, created in Christ Jesus for good works, which God prepared beforehand, that we should walk in them"* Ephesians 2:10 (ESV).

The warmth of a smile is a great place to begin to show a child the difference Christ can make in life. Children are longing to be smiled on. What they may not realize is that Father God is reaching out to them through you, to be His hands, His feet, and His smile. *"Our mouths were filled with laughter, our tongues with songs of joy. Then it was said among the nations, 'The LORD has done great things for them.' The LORD has done great things for us, and we are filled with joy"* Psalm 126:2-3 (NIV).

With all the inevitable traumas attached to childhood, the church must counter culture with the true happiness and peace that only comes from Jesus. Engaging evangelistic endeavors require making a first and lasting impression represented with eye contact and a genuine smile. *"A cheerful look brings joy to the heart; good news makes for good health"* Proverbs 15:30 (NLT).

Friendliness and kindness are two key attributes that are evidenced by a smile. Without these two partners running throughout your ministry and written all over your face, the sincerity and authenticity that kids pick up on immediately, will fall short. A smile speaks a universal language. It embraces ethnicity, social differences, language barriers, and varying degrees of life–inflicted pain and disillusions.

"Smile, it is the key that fits the lock of everybody's heart."
- Anthony D' Angelo.

I fondly recall my school music teacher donning a mask of funny mustache with springy eyes in the middle of a Kiwanis Festival choir performance. Hidden from the serious, prim, and proper adjudicators, he successfully managed to bring smiles to our mass choir and we brought home a first place prize that year! Whether you're connecting one-on-one with a child or leading a large group of children, a smile is worth a thousand words!

What kind of smile are you wearing? Is it a toothless grin, spread with wide abandon? Are you gluing it on, to cover up another long and tiring week? Smearing it on and rushing through the busyness and hindrances to true ministry? Are you plastering or chiseling it on, hoping it doesn't crack under the pressure of another rough day? Or is your smile upside down, hinting at a strange yet somewhat familiar contest between gratitude and grumpiness? Are your smile lines deep and wide, from healthy overuse? Or are worry lines etching themselves more than skin deep?

It's been said that a smile can "cover a multitude of sins." So ideally, in your own presentation of ministry to children, a smile can also cover the multitude of so-called imperfections that you may be obsessing over. A low budget, a lack of volunteer or executive support, the absence of the latest technology or trendy curriculums, can all seem insurmountable! Let your own discouragement be thwarted by a smile. Shine that smile big and large. *"If I say, 'I will forget my complaint, I will change my expression, and smile'"* Job 9:27 (NLT).

Don't allow the obstacles of stress, discouragement, and hurriedness in your ministry interfere with the smile, greeting families at the door for check-in, or undermine the enthusiastic delivery in large group worship, praising with a smile. Storytellers and small group shepherds take heart and share your heart with a grin! *"So, my very dear friends, don't get thrown off course. Every desirable and beneficial gift comes out of heaven. The gifts are rivers of light cascading down from the Father of Light. There is nothing deceitful in God, nothing two-faced, nothing fickle. He brought us to life using the true Word, showing us off as the crown of all his creatures"* James 1:17-18 (MSG).

Your creator, the Father of Lights, wants to spend time with you. He wants to smile on you for a while each day. Take the time to bask in His presence; let the light of His face shine on you. Let the effects of His most powerful and delightful light be mirrored in you! And after you spend time in His presence, His smile becomes your smile. And your God-given smile powerfully impacts the people you come in contact with. *"Make your face shine on your servant; save me in your steadfast love!"* Psalm 31:16 (NLT).

I've always treasured the lines of this song, made popular by Phillips, Craig, and Dean. It reminds me that it is the light of Jesus' face that gives us the capacity to smile through pain and laugh at the things to come.

"Lord let your light, light of your face shine on us.
Lord let your light, light of your face shine on us.
That we may be saved, that we may have life,
to find our way in the darkest night,
Let your light shine on us."

—Michael W Smith, Deborah Smith

In my own life, smiling has not come easily. Many people I come in contact with have wondered at my ability to smile and be truly happy. My husband, Carlos, and I became first-time parents 18 years ago. However, our new parent smiles were interrupted by the greatest challenge we have faced. The loss of our beautiful first-born, full-term and 4-day-old baby girl, Susannah Andrea, was devastating for us. The syndrome I passed to her claimed her life as she was born without kidneys, a bladder, and underdeveloped lungs. Being born with Ectodermal Dysplasia Syndrome with Cleft Lip and Palate has caused lifelong physical and social challenges for me due to facial difference, speech, hearing and dental issues, and syndactyl of the fingers. As we raise our now three children, two of whom also inherited the syndrome, we face daily physical, social, and financial challenges. Yet, through all of these struggles, from childhood to motherhood, my smile has always returned to me, because of Jesus. I have learned that Jesus turns my sorrow into dancing, my pain into joy. I've learned to allow the light of His smile fill my life and to seek comfort and strength from the Great Comforter, the Holy Spirit. *"Count it all joy, my brothers, when you meet trials of various kinds, for you know that the testing of your faith produces steadfastness, And let steadfastness have its full effect, that you may be perfect and complete, lacking in nothing"* James 1:2-4 (NLT).

Remember today to turn over your sorrow and pain to Christ. Whatever roadblocks you're facing in your life and ministry, lay them down and embrace the anointing that God has placed upon you as a kidmin! You are anointed of God to share the light of a smile with His precious little ones. His supernatural power is the one and only source from which you will be able to overcome the trials of this life, to rise above, to reach out and turn your story of pain to deliverance into someone else's message of hope. *"The Spirit of God, the Master, is on me because God anointed me. He sent me to preach good news to the poor, heal the heartbroken, announce freedom to all captives, and pardon all prisoners. God sent me to announce the year of his grace—a celebration of God's destruction of our enemies—and to comfort all who mourn. To care for the needs of all who mourn in Zion, give them bouquets of roses instead of ashes, messages of joy instead of news of doom, a praising heart instead of a languid spirit. Rename them 'Oaks of Righteousness' planted by God to display his glory. They'll rebuild the old ruins; raise a new city out of the wreckage. They'll start over on the ruined cities, take the rubble left behind and make it new. You'll hire outsiders to herd your flocks and foreigners to work your fields, but you'll have the title 'Priests of God,' honored as ministers of our God. You'll feast on the bounty of nations; you'll bask in their glory. Because you got a double dose of trouble and more than your share of contempt, your inheritance in the land will be doubled and your joy go on forever"* Isaiah 61:3 (MSG).

Your smile is connected to your ears. As you smile and welcome children and families into the Kingdom of God, you must listen to hear a child's story and gain a sense of his or her needs.

Are you aware of the unique delivery the children in your ministry will need in order to learn and embrace the message of Jesus?

Your smiling face is connected to your shoulders, arms, and hands. My own children's amazing kindergarten teacher has offered her students every day for years, as they finish out each school day, "Do you want a hug, a handshake, or a high five?" From a gentle touch to a hearty hug, whichever you choose to give, it qualifies for the physical contact every child yearns for!

And as you are reminded in the old spiritual song, "Dem Bones" written by James Weldon Johnson, your smiling face eventually connects to the knee bones. You must position yourself at eye level with children, so they can always see the light of a smile on your face—the reflection of Christ.

A smile will take you miles in ministry but the strength of one hundred smiles will take you ten thousand ministry miles! Surround yourself with kidmin team leaders and volunteers who are like-minded—individuals who want to reflect Christ's smile and whom have found the joy of the Lord to truly be the strength of their lives. They have received that beam of light you call a smile!

As you endeavor to energize, engage, and equip children, remember your Smile Science and keep it simple as a smile!

Jennifer Osmond Escalante has been wearing a smile for 40-something years, overcoming physical and social roadblocks such as facial difference and hearing loss for both herself and for three of her four children. Serving as an early childhood educator and children's pastor, Jennifer and her husband, Carlos, reside in Calgary, Alberta, Canada and enjoy ministering smiles with their children through their home-based, JCSQUAD Family Ministries.

CPSIA information can be obtained
at www.ICGtesting.com
Printed in the USA
FFOW02n0622180518
46743610-48879FF